The culture of your pe

The Defence of Lawino

Okot p'Bitek

A new translation of *Wer pa Lawino*
by
Taban lo Liyong

Fountain Publishers

Wer pa Lawino was first published in 1969 by the East African Publishing
House, Nairobi, Kenya

Fountain Publishers Ltd
P.O. Box 488
Kampala

© *Wer pa Lawino* 1969: Okot p'Bitek
© Translation (*The Defence of Lawino*): Taban lo Liyong 2001
First published 2001

ISBN 9970 02 269 5

Dedications

I am grateful to my buddy Olobo Abucu Stephen, my friend Acamu Too son of Lubwa and his help-meet 'ma-in-law' Ayiko Anna; bro-in-law Abonga Bongomin Lutwala and his partner, mother-in-law Auma Yayeri, my uncle Padre Okelo Antonio; youth-leader Anywar son of Latim, Moore Gerald a whiteman, Beloved brother Lawoko Apolo Wod' Okelo; my nephew Ocieng' son of Lakana Jany and his good wife; my sister-in-law Aol Lily and companion Oloya Silvano for the deep love that binds us together and for assisting and urging me to persevere in composing the *Song of Lawino*.

The author
Okot p'Bitek

Wer pa Lawino was dedicated

to
Auma Kalina Kireng

by the author
Okot p'Bitek

Contents

v

Foreword

The historical trajectory of *Te Okono Obur Bong Luputu: Wer par Lawino* is our most obvious starting point. In his introduction, Taban lo Liyong suggests that this Acholi song has been in existence since 1949, and was published by the East African Publishing House in 1969. It is a sobering observation when one considers the often invisible world of indigenous literatures in Africa. By contrast, in mapping the cartographies of African Literature, it is usual to begin with Chinua Achebe's *Things Fall Apart* (with a sideswipe at Amos Tutuola), published a full ten years after Okot's homage to our common African heritage. Like Ochol, we are wilfully complicit in its denigration. While texts written in English attain immediate acclaim, the lack of translations from one African language into another forces us to remain apart until the white man, in his benevolence, brings us together. This is the painful reality. Wonderful literature continues to flourish in countries such as Tanzania, where the issue of the Aids epidemic has been imaginatively grappled with using easily accessible technology such as the radio and dramatising a truck driver's woes. In South Africa we would rather throw R14 million away staging plays that ignore rural communities. Squandering our limited resources by shunning indigenous languages in favour of 'the bigger the better' theory of looting the state is one legacy apartheid has left to fester in the present, despite routine fulminations from Parliament.

Flowing from the above, the battle for an African literary re-awakening (renaissance) can never be separated from orature. More than anyone, Okot p' Bitek realised that only by 'returning to the source' - to use Aimé Césaire's wonderful phrase - could we 're-discover the ordinary', and hence our truer selves. His deeply philosophical outlook seeks to re-connect us to that which we lose on a daily basis by hankering after European culture. Take the rhythmic outlook Africans infuse in telling the seasons: the beauty of Lawino's understanding of the seasons compares favourably with the Tswanan calendar from which the month of Powane ('a young bull') had to be dropped.

According to Bessie Head, during this month young bulls sharpened their horns to prepare themselves for fights of the mating season. After a few showers had fallen, they thrust their horns into wet ant-hills to sharpen them. Or take another contentious example of our wilful self-blinding: African cosmology does not dream of closure, for we are not an island people. Living on this vast continent, our ancestors made a world view that knew no end, hence there is no sense in insisting that the spirit world and the living world are separate. In rejecting such a philosophical basis of ourselves, we have plucked the pumpkin from the old homesteads. Culture, as lo Liyong reminds us, is *Rutan*:folk-knowledge.

It is fitting that this offering from a man of letters reverberates with inter-textuality, and we should expect no less. As a crowning reminder at the close of this contentious century, this addition to African literature re-positions itself in the long tradition that has had as close an affinity with our reawakening as nothing else produced on the continent. For in an attempt to re-assemble the broken gourds of our abandoned ancestral homesteads, the artist as ruler had to lead the way. If the land was not immediately recoverable because of the presence of the coloniser, it had to be first imagined that way. This painstaking translation, nineteen years in the making and echoing Lawino's indignation, disgust, bafflement, and defiant spirit, profoundly revisits issues raised in texts such as Sol Plaatje's *Mhudi*, Chinua Achebe's *Arrow of God*, Ngugi wa Thiong'o's *The River Between*, Ingoapele Madingoane's *afrika my beginning*, Modikwe Dikobe's *Marabi Dance,* and Ferdinand Oyono's *Houseboy*. Yet, elder that he is, lo Liyong does not stop there: a perceptive reader will realise hints of Toni Morrison's wonderful woman of the egg in *Tar Baby*, and allusions to Salman Rushdie's *The Satanic Verses*. Nothing exercises the reader's mind more than to see the broad range of Lawino's concerns, concerns that we need to grapple with as we enter the unknown frontier represented by this calendrical event of the new millennium.

Lawino's Submissions will haunt us as we journey into the unknown. For we have, through Ochol, forgotten the riches in our homesteads: the use of *lelwala*, for instance, to rub a pregnant woman's tummy and thus ease the parturition pains, the use of *lekgala/intelezi* in all matters pertaining to our own health (which, horror of horrors, comes back to us in the form of aloe products from Europe); it is these that make us mimic people in Lawino's eyes. In our ignorance, we have blissfully forgotten that our ancestors had cosmetic products, were fanatical about hygiene, had different and various hairstyles, took part in dances to celebrate the exuberance of life, knew of various child care remedies, had a vast knowledge of the bounty of the forests around the dwellings, and culinary tastes second to none. Only recently it has been 'discovered' that for centuries Malaysian women used a certain tea as a preventive measure against pregnancy. Who then dares to say we, like our counterparts in the so-called 'third world', had no culture? If we but repent, like Ochol, we can re-make ourselves from the pyrrhic victory of a turbulent century. Lawino's gaze shames us. Much like Christopher Okigbo, we need to return to Mother Idoto and, naked, confess our sins of omission, beg forgiveness and perform the necessary rites of purification as demanded in Submission Thirteen.

It would be presumptuous of me to speak of the literary merits of the *The Defence of Lawino*. That I leave to those more knowledgeable than myself. I do know, however, that it will give immense pleasure to those who are painfully aware of and deeply concerned with the problems afflicting Mother Africa. Sons of lo Liyong, I salute you. May your spear never rest, like the thirteen offensives launched against our enemies so many moons ago! May that spear always find the target, for this cannot be the last word! Despite time's advancement, the battle is not yet won, the homesteads must be repaired, using any means necessary!

It is a great honour to write a foreword to this offering from our elder, Professor of Letters, Taban lo Liyong.

S. Raditlhalo
University of the North
Republic of South Africa

ix

Preface

A

In 1969, the East African Publishing House, Nairobi, published Okot p'Bitek's excellent Acholi language poem called *Wer pa Lawino*. In its full title, there is a proverbial preface: *Te Okono Obur Bong Luputu: Wer pa Lawino*. Loosely translated, it means: Lawino's thesis: The Culture of Your People You Don't Abandon. The whole exercise was therefore philosophical, and deeply infused with anthropological knowledge, defence of Acholi and (by extension) therefore African indigenous culture.

Lawino, an intelligent and traditionally cultured village girl stood for all that was good, seemly and enduring in our indigenous culture. She is therefore revolted at the desertion of those very values by her husband, a young prince, who had gone to school, and who should have known better. Instead of her husband Ochol using school education to add wisdom to the Acholi outlook on life, and to sharpen his mind in choices of cultural artefacts, (modern) gadgets and practices that were to be made during the European colonial and religious era, he senselessly went for evolving into a Christian Black Englishman.

In *Te Okono Obur Bong Luputu: Wer pa Lawino*, we hear Lawino's part of the story. Her husband wants to divorce her. Although he does not speak directly to the readers, Lawino reports his reasons for seeking to put her aside. In her spirited defence, Lawino then produces Ochol's charges and reasons in the various themes of human life in which he alleges African ways are inadequate, and then proceeds to devastate them. *Te Okono Obur Bong Luputu: Wer pa Lawino* therefore integrates Okot's knowledge of social anthropology, the religions and culture of Central Lwo, education, and law.

Before composing *Wer pa Lawino* (in short) in Acholi language, Okot had written *Lak Tar Miyo Kinyero Wi Lobo: We laugh in order to show our white teeth* in Acholi language. But, that was when the East African Literature Bureau was encouraging writing and publishing in the various vernaculars of East Africa. Though this trend resembled that vigorously put into operation by apartheid forces in Southern and Central Africa, on the positive side it also helped to preserve African languages and cultures.

Now, when Anglophone literature became popular, especially after Heinemann had launched its African Writers Series, and after the Writer's Workshop in Makerere in 1962, for which only writers in English and French were invited, Okot had to translate *Te Okono Obur Bong Luputu: Wer pa Lawino* into *the Song of Lawino.*

It must have broken Lawino's heart to see her song now presented in the language her husband despises her in, in the language of the culture that was oppressing her, to see herself defeated. (But, I think the defeat was (and still is) a pyrrhic victory). The debate for the primacy of African culture in Africa is an ongoing debate. The future of African culture is bright especially after the ineptitude of the independence oligarchs and the pressure of rival Asian values and cultures to fill the space of dominance the colonisers had forcefully hollowed out of us.

Song of Lawino (the English language version) is not strictly a faithful translation of *Wer pa Lawino*. It is a version, if you like, of *Wer pa Lawino* in which, whatever was topical, striking, graphic and easily renderable into English received due prominence. But the darker, more ponderous, more intricate parts, or those nuances that only the best *nanga* (harp) players know how to reproduce, suffered summarising or mutilation. Or new recasting.

So, word by word, line by line, even chapter by chapter, *Song of Lawino* is a watered down, lighter, elaborated, extended version of *Wer pa Lawino*.

Now, in 1992, which is the tenth anniversary of Okot's untimely death in 1982, as well as the twenty-second year of my initiating this translation of *Wer pa Lawino*, (started on March 14, 1970), I have had the hindsight to deduce the main thrusts of Lawino's themes and to restate them in this new era of linguistic, religious and economic dominance. And what I found out is that Lawino's song was her (and our) defence of indigenous African ways. And I had to restate them as her 'submissions' before the council of elders that she had specifically summoned for such a purpose in stanza four of Submission One: "My people, I am appealing to you, please hear my case". But since Lawino knows everything, she is the accuser throughout, as well as the judge at the end and the pronouncer of absolutions. If only her husband admitted his errors, repented, accepted exorcism of the daemons of colonisation that had produced temporary amnesia in him he could be made whole again. So appeals Lawino.

But, will Ochol wisen up, get whole again, and take up his manly legitimate defence of African culture? That is the big question. And since in our various ways we are versions of Ochol, perhaps we should study again what negritude was all about.

B

I started translating *Te Okono Obur Bong Luputu: Wer pa Lawino*, into English on March 14th, 1970 in August Moon cafeteria in Nairobi. My favourite chapter was 12, followed by 2; then came 13, 9, and 14. I worked on it on and off in December 1981; September 1982 (in Juba); and December 1991 and August 18th 1992 when I completed the whole translation in Khartoum. Additional revisions were made to the whole draft in Perth, Australia, November 1994. And final touches were made in October and November 1998 in Venda, South Africa.

Since I embarked on the translation, I have never revisited Okot p'Bitek's *Song of Lawino* at all. I wanted my translation to bear the burden of Lawino's Acholi version and not to be coloured by Okot's mannerisms and poetics of translation. I would have cheated if I had tried to rework Okot's version but not ventured to make my own.

It is a pity that Okot passed away in 1982 when he was moving into personal and original philosophising. For Lawino's philosophy is the wisdom of the ancestors compiled and thematically parcelled by Okot p'Bitek. (Just like Chinua Achebe's early trilogy is the voice and wisdom of the ancestors and not necessarily his own personal original philosophy. Granted, of course, that his choice of themes and casting of them displayed his philosophical tendencies). Of course Okot's personality and judgement guided him in what to see, how to arrange it, and how to state it. But it is in *Artist the Ruler* that Okot now starts to state his own thesis: artists are the rulers.It is very much like Percy Bysshe Shelley's thesis that poets are the unacknowledged legislators of the world. But Okot's is more embrasive. It includes (as artists) - smiths, orators, dancers, builders, novelists, etc. Because they tinker away in their smithies, studios, studies then come out with new artefacts, tools, ideas, outlooks, interpretations which society adopts and popularises and uses they are the rulers.

By using the products of artists, society acknowledges its subjection to the 'rule' of artists.Unfortunately when he wrote it - *Artist the Ruler* - he was now wrestling with the ghosts of the American educational philosopher John Dewey and some other English and continental religious philosophers. These are the 'ghosts' whose books filled Ochol's study. But, perhaps Okot had started going astray the moment he agreed to write *Song of Ochol*. Instead of Lawino's thesis being his philosophical thesis - as Voltaire's optimism was exemplified in *Candide*, the demonstration of Pangloss's philosophy - Okot now treated it as a mere song against which the anti-thesis (Ochol's rejoinder) could be penned by the same author.

On the tenth anniversary of his death, we arrived at the crossroads where his former colleagues were going their own philosophical ways. Professor Ali al Amin Mazrui has now retreated from Kenyan-ness (if ever he had it), from Africanity, into Islam and Pan-Arabism. He thinks the Red Sea is an aberration, a trick, played by colonial demons to separate Oman from Africa. Professor John Mbiti is still convinced that Christianity is the highest religion in the world - it offers absolution by faith in the martyred Master Jesus. Ngugi wa Thiong'o has woken up to the love of Gikuyu language which he would like to draft into the service of international socialism and new nationalism for the Kikuyu and, later, for Kenyans.

On my part, I advocate not only the use of the vernacular, but much more so, the use of the vernacular for restating and stating the innermost thoughts in indigenous cultures. In other words, the return to African languages alone is not enough. We should return to African languages to use them as paradigms and lenses for seeing much more clearly the inner meaning and strength of African culture. We should, through African languages, explore the old homesteads where the pumpkins are still growing and re-establish or plant or retransplant the cultures of the old homesteads in our new homesteads. It is therefore with that urgency in mind that I have been writing most of my essays and the translation of this *Defence of Lawino* is, in a way, my own defence too, as well as justification.

C

Both my *Defence of Lawino* and Okot p'Bitek's *Song of Lawino* come from *Wer pa Lawino*. That poem in Acholi was 20 years old when it was published by East African Publishing House in 1969. The last version was an improvement on the 1956 version. When I was a pupil in Sir Samuel Baker School (where Okot was our Biology teacher!) in 1955, he read parts of it to us. The Acholi *Wer pa Lawino* is a rhymed poem from the first line to the last. The predominant rhyme scheme is end rhyme of the aba bcb cdc ded efe... terza rima variety. Though in one passage there is a riot of aaaaaaaaa... Though there was no conscious attempt at metric composition, there is a rhythm and the lines average eight syllables; some go beyond ten. But, on the whole, the lines are longer than those in *Song of Lawino,* and they are more ponderous, and the thoughts therein are more measured.

The Christian hymn-book in Acholi and *Song of Hiawatha*, no doubt, influenced its composition. But when I was a student in Gulu High School (before going to Sir Samuel Baker School) we were told in no uncertain terms by our English teacher that poems RHYME. Okot was there before me. Some of my other teachers also attempted poetry composition in Acholi language and they all had end rhymes.Because he had to use end rhymes, he had to stretch the Acholi language to its limits in order to squeeze rhyming words out of it. He used the standard orthography of Acholi language, as well as the quaint and archaic dialects of east and north Acholi. He also used the joking register of youth a lot - remember Lawino is talking about their days of youth? Okot also used the sub-dialect of the country bums just come to town who dropped their aiches and swallowed their end syllables.

Words from neighbouring sub-languages - Lango, Alur, Jonam, Jo-Palwo - all these Lwo dialects contributed to the enrichment of the Acholi language. Since Acholi youth had also gone to fight in the Second World War, learning enough Swahili to obey orders, they came back home priding themselves on their little Swahili. This is included in *Wer pa Lawino*, particularly abusive words, barking, ordering words from military life. Gulu also has Nubi-speakers - Ki-Nubi being the Arabic pidgin used by the remnants of Emin Pasha's soldiers who were later on inherited by Lord Lugard and utilised to 'pacify' or subjugate Uganda. Thus, a few words from Luganda, English, and catechistic words and formulas in Latin, found their way in *Wer pa Lawino*.Okot read anthropology at Oxford. They denied him the D.Phil.

I think he had presented the wrong thesis. Had he presented *Wer pa Lawino* I would have called the Oxonian dons dumb fools who did not know the depth of cultural understanding that Okot had put into it. *Wer pa Lawino* is deep philosophy.Unfortunately, the depth of thought, the body of the poem, thinned in the translation into Okot's *Song of Lawino*. He confessed in the English preface to having "clipped the eagle's feather," therefore reducing its soaring powers.I would not have minded that, but he went for drama, humour, and the striking figures of speech. Whereas *Wer pa Lawino* does not excite laughter in every other line, that hidden sarcasm that was muted in Acholi language came to the fore when Okot was addressing not only Clementina the ape, but the object to be aped: the white woman and man who had destroyed the pride of Acholi woman and the dignity of the Acholi prince.

Song of Lawino is addressed more to the English and English-speaking Africans. It is graphic, and has a more biting satire and the lines are even fewer. Of course end-rhymes disappeared. There is rhythm and the beauty of the original gives it whatever lustre that still shines through.My version, *The Defence of Lawino*, tries as faithfully as possible to reproduce Lawino's thoughts in as rhythmic an English as suits her mode of discourse. The original rhyme scheme (most times abab, but sometimes aa or aaaaa.... depending on availability of rhyming words) both Okot and I have dispensed with. Curiously, Okot had imported English (it was actually American, fashioned after Henry Wadsworth Longfellow's *Song of Hiawatha* with a huge licence) rhyme into Acholi. But when we rendered her thoughts into English we had to settle for rhythm. It is a pity really. For the beauty of *Wer pa Lawino* comes about mostly because of the way Okot had brought to rhyme a variety of words from Acholi dialects with Bantu, English, and Ki-Nubi thrown in for good measure. So, since most of the "poetry" in *Wer pa Lawino* is the trope provided by the rhyming words, any translation would not do the original work justice.

But, Okot's topical, graphic, and exciting version, read side by side with my ponderous explanatory lines, should yield to the reader as much of what the Acholi original has as is possible. Since I started translating *Wer pa Lawino*, I have never looked at Okot's *Song of Lawino* again. I have tried to return the discussion to where it was: Lawino discoursing on African ways of life to fellow Africans without too much consciousness about the presence of the whites. I have, I hope, maintained the philosophical tone, the gravity of the original, but supplied my own rhythm, which permitted my English version to be orally deliverable. Although my translation is not strictly line-by-line, I tried to be faithful to the sense, spirit, and complexity of the total poem in order to bring out the nuances that are found *in Wer pa Lawino*.

When faced with the dilemma of elucidating a point prosaically or recasting the point poetically, I have opted for rendering meaning rather than soaring poetically. This is particularly so in "Submission Eight" which is biographical but "Submission Nine" which is bantering par excellence gave me wings to soar. I have translated and included chapter fourteen. Chapter Fourteen? In *Song of Lawino* there is no Chapter Fourteen. I asked Okot what had happened? He said he was exhausted after translating Chapter Thirteen. My Chapter Fourteen (Submission Fourteen) is the only conclusion of *Wer pa Lawino* in English. With it, the various threads that were left loose are brought together. Even some of my earlier criticisms of *Song of Lawino* which I had made as I read through the book the first time now get answered.

Finally, though I had started this translation as a challenge when my social and intellectual colleague was alive, I finished it as a duty to the dead. *The Defence of Lawino* is my remembrance of Okot p'Bitek as well as my way of keeping in touch and continuing the discussion about our old homesteads, our pumpkins and their embrasive tendrils.

Don't rest, Okot. The war is not yet won!

Taban lo Liyong,
Venda
Republic of South Africa

xvi

My husband calls me names and abuses my parents too because we uphold African ways

My husband, though you still despise me
My man, though you still abuse me
Claiming that I have inherited the clumsiness of my aunt;
Beloved prince, though you reduce me
Comparing me to the rubbish in the refuse heap;
Though you cheapen me, broadcasting that you like
    me no more
Claiming that I am equal to debris left in the deserted home;
Though you abuse me, and do it shamelessly,
Claiming it is because I don't even know 'a'
And that I have not got school education
And that I have not even got a baptism name;
You compare me to pups, making senseless noise;

Take care my friend, my brother's age-mate
Control your tongue, man, watch your tongue
Think about the deeper meanings of things
For you are now a man, and not a moron
It is unbecoming of you to behave like a child.

Bear this in mind, Ochol you are a true prince
And should leave role-playing to kids:
It is a shame to hear you rebuked in songs.
Desist from foolishly disgracing people
Don't treat me as if I was the ashen salt-less slag.
Grow up, become mature, and leave foolish things alone.
The deep roots of our culture, who has ever uprooted them?

1

My people, I am appealing to you, please hear my case:
The abuses men give women pain us deeply:
My husband calls me names, and abuses my parents too,
He hurls unseemly abuses even at my mother
He defames me in foreign tongues, and unashamedly says
That I am a half-wit so he doesn't like me:
He even calls my mother's private parts by name, making
    me ashamed:

He censures me for not knowing how to play the guitar;
He claims I am blind, my eyes are mere sockets that can't read.
He says I can't write, and my ears are blocked;
That I don't know the English tongue, and can't reckon
    money well
He says I resemble the sheep, one as foolish as the other;
He treats me as if I were not a human being
He insists I am as foolish as the flies that feed on beer dregs.

Ochol hits me badly with his abuses:
Spoken words pain more than blows.
He casts a slur on his mother-in-law, saying that she's a witch
He says my uncle's people are fools: they feed on rats;
He condemns all our people as pagan-believers
Who do not know the way of the Christian God;
He claims we dwell in darkness, unlit by *Evangeli*
He claims my mother weaves her talisman in her lace of shells
He avers we're all bewitchers, we're not yet converted.

My husband's tongue is bitter like the lily flesh
It is hot like the sting of bees, or black ant's bite
Like the scorpion's sting, or the barren woman's potion,
Ochol's tongue is as bitter as the calabash fruit.

*   *   *

Whenever my husband has warmed up to despising the blacks
He stirs up as much dust as the careless hen

2

That should be locked up in a cage.
He works himself up and shouts till his eyes are red
Till they're as red as those of the electric fish!
He would hit wild like the large hyena cornered by hunters;
He would behave wilder than the wildest beast.
His favourite theses are these: African cultures are bad;
All black people are backward, they're still left behind;
That African dances are deadly sins;
All blacks are fools, their knowledge is small;
Unlike him who is a civilised man
That he's an educated modern man;
The man of the hour, up-to-date in every way;
He has read deep and wide
It lowers his dignity to have me for a wife
Who is unable to judge between good and bad;
He says, being a person from the bush, what do I know?
He says I am a relic from the past, pitiable to behold,
That his march forward is hindered by having me around;
That my big head resembles the elephant's
There is no brain in it; it is an empty case;
He says my brain is as tiny as a swallow's
My husband concludes that continued stay with me wastes
    his time!

My husband now rejects me and loves his new wife who apes European ways

Ochol my husband now hates me and loves someone modern
His darling wife is she who talks in 'Gut', 'No'.
There was a time when we sat body-touching-body
There were days when I praised him on my lyre;
When he used to swear I am his only respected one
When he cowed me with sweet-sounding English words!

Ochol has turned against the old and fallen for the new
He is in hot pursuit of some girl who has been to school,
The said beauty goes by the name Clementine.

Oh brother, had you beheld the said Clementine
What a beauty in white apemanship!
Her mouth glows red like live embers;
Her lips are red like a beast's after drinking blood;
Her red mouth protrudes like cancerous growth,
It looks ulcerous, like a ghost's mouth!

Clementine heaps powder all over her face,
    looking deadly pale
Like a witch on the verge of his nightly trips
To dance naked, obscene, and unseemly.
When unworthy women resort to affectation
They grab at straws and heap ashes all over their faces
Then when in anger they begin to perspire
Streams of sweat course down their faces, making
    them resemble fowls.

4

A sorry sight. But I am not despising her.
Using powder does me no good; it brings me nervous
    breakdowns

I become sickly, each time I smell jayce soap it makes me sickly.
Powder does not agree with me; it makes me sick
Necessitating the bringing of the avuncular sacrificial goat,
The beating of the ritual drum, and the exorcism dance.

I am allergic to powdering my face;
It is a thing that suits Europeans: they are already ashen-white.
But when a black girl heaps dust on her face
She looks sickly pale: her royal highness looks bad
Even though she were a paragon, long necked.

Powder chemicals have corroded Clementine's face;
Her forehead is bleached, there are brown patches here and there
As if burnt by rainbow, or struck by lightning flash
The skin of her face looks like a babe's.
To her, that's the thing: the nearest she can get to being white.
Her face is freckled, she looks like the hyena:
Her neck and arms still look nice like ours.

Clementine looks like a person burnt by fire,
Like the bush-buck burnt in a raging grass fire;
Starting with her mouth swollen red like yaws;
And her overgrown hair, with hair standing out like an owl's
The head looks like a worm-eater's, like a wizard's,
Like an imbecile's which cries out for psychiatric healing.
Especially as her neck is long and thin, her eyes pale and wan.

Forgive me, dear reader, I beg you
Don't think I am abusing my rival, no;
Or that my tongue waxes grand because of anger, no:
The sight of Clementine makes me pity her.

5

I won't deny I am prey to being jealous
I won't deceive you: we all get jealous once in a while;
Jealousy strikes you all of a sudden like a fit.
It hits you unannounced like an earth tremor.
But, jealousy aside, Tina is a pity to behold!

The new wife's breasts are so flat, so emaciated:
They are mere cartilage, mine are full compared to them.
She makes bird's nests out of cotton
Then carefully folds her leathery breasts into them.

Marvel at the tricks modern women use to look young!
Lets give praise to white people for being so resourceful
For, had they not invented the useful bra
Kele would have had a flat chest like a boy's;
And, had we no addicts in make-believe
My rival's chest would have resembled an asthmatic's.

If there were no frocks to cover bony hips,
For wrapping up weak ribs that stick out;
If there were no gunny sacks for beefing up flat buttocks
With blankets used to fleshen up twiggy waists
If the *gomes* dress were not there to cover lumbar regions
To keep out of sight protruding calluses
Many women would be lost, would hide from sight.

The bra is moulded to a point
To prick the chests of men like darts.
Husband Ochol, my man, you've been hoodwinked!
This sister of mine, how many kids has she had, I wonder?
Her breasts were flattened by children's suckling, I swear!
How many abortions has she had, I ask?
She looks like those women who drop foetuses into pit latrines!

Is this new wife really a first-time wife?
Might Kele not be a divorcee?

Or an old spinster who has aged at home?
This age-mate of my mother's looks like a former wife
    elsewhere!

My husband-sharer walks like a person whose life-force
    is detained
Like a ghost, she walks without audible steps!
There is no enthusiasm in anything Tina does:
All said, she is incapable of feast-cooking for a crowd.
She looks sickly, but it is actually hunger!
She doesn't eat, claiming food makes her fat!
She claims the doctor's order is for her not to eat
She's now twiggy, her bones rattle as she walks.
Her lips jut out, red like red robin's chest
The waist is contracted like a wasp's, she's so flat
She's thin and emaciated like a lunatic
The new wife is compressed flat like an insect.
Ochol has brought home an item of no value.

*   *   *

But my man is wrapped up in his dream life;
He laughs at me, heaping scorn,
Claiming he's above me in every way:
He has no use for me; he cares not a jot for me
It degrades him to be called my man,
As if I am not a human being even!

Ochol claims he's not the age-mate of my grannies
To be saddled with a wife who has not been to school,
He claims I lack sense
Since I have never been to school
He mocks me openly, with no reservations,
He's puffed up with the pride of children playing with toys;
Publicly my man declares aloud
That I am equal in every way to my grandma
Who wraps herself in cow-hide to sleep
Therefore he could not be my man.

*   *   *

7

I have no ill-feelings against my man
I do not restrain him from having another wife:
Be she a nubile girl or an aged divorcee!
Who can ever stop men loving women?
Who has ever discovered the cure for thirst,
Or hunger-killer, anger-depressant, anti-lust pill?
In the dry season the sun shines: rain falls in the wet season
Women hunt for men, men seek out women.
I am elated when my husband has married another wife
The co-wife who is jealous of her fellow wife
Is she who is sullen or who is bashful;
Is she who's cold-blooded, who cannot roast nuts for a journey
Is she who's weak and utterly careless.

For, you compete for a man's favours by taking him pipe fire
When he's returned from the field or hunting ground;
You compete in taking him drinking water or seasoned
    porridge first
Whichever wife emerges first with the meal of the day
Whose cookery deserves the palates of chiefs
Who is sprightly, unlike some ancient hag,
Whose food comes piping hot, whose owner enjoys her role
Who enjoys company, whose mind is clear, heart's clean,
    whose eyes are bright
Who is generous and shares her food with friends;
She who enjoys jokes, is good humoured and does not brood
Who is witty, sharp in repartee and doesn't anger quickly
She who isn't grave and not periodically covered in dark moods
Such is the wife who enjoys the husband's trust.

I do not stop my husband loving his wife,
If he wants, let him build for her a mansion on the mountain top,
That is none of my affairs, I do not hate her,
My thatched hut is still good enough for me.

I am not angry with my counter-wife
For I do not fear to compete with her:
Mere housework cannot kill me;
Each person knows her scope.

But I wish Ochol refrained from abusing me
He should not abuse nor cheapen us
He should not cover his ignorance in arguments
He should not babble and give it out that I am inept,
Or abuse me together with the mother who bore me,
Or look down on African ways and call them ugly
He should stop toddling and staggering in the ways
      of other people
For it makes one wonder on what poisoned milk his
      mother fed him
Or if he had hired parents to bring him up!

*   *   *

Stop despising us, my man, don't look down on us,
Africans have traditions that are good
Don't fool yourself that your ways are bad
African cultures are solid, not hollow,
Neither thin, nor weak, nor light and flimsy.

But Ochol, although you have read up to university
You are big for nothing, you have no weight
You cannot guide us, addicted as you are
To copying foreign ways
As if your people have none of their own:
We have nothing to expect from you now
You deserve a beating for your loose tongue.

The cultures of other people I do not despise:
Don't you look down upon your own;
Borrowed stuff can never become your staple food
Don't uproot the culture of your land.

My husband rejects me because I do not know or love European dances (I have my reasons!)

The dances of foreigners, truly speaking, I do not know.
Their dresses too are unknown to me,
Even the games foreigners play still defeat me;
But in the dances of our people dances that are artful I am adept.

In attempting the *rumba* dance I will trip myself up,
My mother brought me up since childhood on Acholi dances.
The new European dances, borrowed and un-satisfying
Including the *samba*, I don't know, to tell the truth.
My forte, since childhood, is in dancing the *orak*:
A new dance, invented by my people:

And when the dance is now at its best, drums going full blast
And the youth of Africa have stirred up dust, and are drunk
    with it:
It is danced with vigour, danced with pride
It is danced with abandon and expresses joy of life.
The teeth are white, rubbed clean with fine sand;
And each girl seeks out a non-relative to captivate.

It is a display of keenness and a teasing competition
It is a mixture of disrespect, altercations or real fights,
The eyes of the boys, spirit-possessed, are already red;
The bull-girl and the he-man would distinguish themselves there;
Slaves and displaced dance apart from native borns.

It is an open challenge, danced with songs:
Songs that are provocative, backbiting and abusive,

10

Some are praise songs, others of woe because of heartbreak.
Most of the songs make one angry;
Only a few are truly love-songs.

It is danced with impertinence and provocation
Nobody comes to dance when already drunk;
When a fellow dancer shoves you aside
You react promptly with a rough voice of anger:
For manliness is displayed in the dancing arena;
To overlook an affront is a permanent loss of face.

The girl who cannot keep step with others
Is lazy, weak and does not finish her chores at home.

You dance when fully adorned in the fitting Acholi attires
There'd be fruit rattles or iron ones on your ankles
(You'll remember not to have eaten too much.)
On your waist there'd be the back-apron; leathern or threaded
Apron made of twine-threads or small white skirt;
I'd adorn my waist with ten rounds of beads
Would have ivory-bangles and others on my hands
My neck would be decked with many rounds of giraffe laces.

*   *   *

Your hair would be newly cut and fashionable
Oil would be generously applied to it so it shines
And you would press the hair evenly round your head
On one side, you'd plant your sweet-heart's comb.

The boys' dress consists of back-leather and front cloth
On their necks they would display the beads of their beloveds
With a choice ostrich feather inserted on your hair
You'd strut about, blowing the horn, trumpet or flute.

*   *   *

Our dances are public performances held during daylight,
In the arena, during the day, without a place for hiding
All manner of fat and constipated tummies,
He with scabies on his protruding buttocks,
People with extended hernia on their flanks,
Spinsters whose breasts are beginning to droop,
Hollow chested men whose owners are despised,
He with a burn scars in private parts
The left-handers who rub the calabash the other way
The scars from tattoos that have messed up the chests,
And the beautiful tattoos beneath the navel,
All the little breasts still peeping out, and the full ones,
All manners of physique are displayed in the dancing arena.

Healthy bodies and neat grooming are seen in the arena;
Exemplar upbringing shows itself in the arena.
And then when she-who-is-second-to-none makes her entrance
Tall, spare and jumpy like a little goat
She would not stand still and let the world whirl around her
But jump here, and move there, and shove you away.

The tattoo patterns on her chest would stand out and glisten,
While those on her waist would shine like the stars
The white of her eye would flash like fire-works
And her ripe breasts would resemble the full moon
So that when her brother's age-mate sees them
Or should the eyes of her brother's would-be brother-in-law
      chance on them
Do you think that that stricken young man would sleep at night?
Do you know what restlessness would churn inside him?

*   *   *

To admit the truth, Ochol, dancing the rumba defeats me:
Clasping one's partner chest-to-chest, embarrasses me

12

Holding tight to a man, in public, I can't do it;
These are acts of shame, my father would support me.
What dance is this you do after getting drunk?
Drunk with European spirits or native gins.
What dance is this danced with eyes closed, without a song
Where everyone is paired up even to non-spouses!
Besides, it is danced indoors, with insufficient light;
With some women held so tight, they nearly choke
Yet they drag on, unashamed, like Europeans.
In the dance hall women yield themselves up to their men
Piercing their chests with their sharp breasts;
Men's cheeks would rub against women's cheeks
Girls' heads would be covered with scarves or done in corn-rows;
The women would throw their arms around their men's necks
And the men would press their women's waists onto themselves,
Their knees would dove-tail so shamelessly
When the record comes to an end, they'd still be aroused
And saunter away, hands deep in trouser pockets!

*   *   *

It is danced without respect for mama and papa
Young girls wrap their hands around fathers in a dance;
Brothers hold tight the waists of their very sisters
People pair anyhow, including sons dragging their mothers
     to the stage.
Cousins just gone through puberty are possible night partners.
Modern girls are hard-headed like the Alero Gods
They spare not their nephews,
They throw their bosoms on their uncles' chests,
They are like Jok Labeja, who does not spare nephews and
     their uncles.
The whole thing is done shamelessly in the Europeans' way:
For, Europeans have no sense of decorum and respect;
In the rumba, the woman is embraced openly, like a European;
And the man moves about with her with their chests glued
     together!

13

The dancers would all smoke cigarettes, like Europeans;
Both women and men: smoke like Europeans;
They would all suck their cheeks, like Europeans;
They would all suck their tongues, like Europeans;
They would lick the saliva from their mouths, like Europeans;
Leaving men's mouths plastered with paints, of Europeans
With which their women had smeared their lips;
The men's teeth would redden from the kisses
Making you wonder if their jaws had been hit
With a big blow. All these acts are unbecoming
To our adults and respectable men: behaving like dogs.

Even the clothes worn are European clothes
They are wrapped and tied up as if in European lands
And they sweat in suits even when it's hot, even in dry seasons
Stalwarts walk covered in woollen suits,
And sweat would freely flow down their spines.
The socks on their feet are woollen, made in England;
There would be vests and undergarments first
Then a shirt and a tie made in England would follow:
Layer after layer of dress would be heaped, as if one were sick
Even the eyes would be compounded with glasses!

Inside the dance hall the stench is thick like a cave:
Women gasp and faint like doped fish;
They stumble left and right and fall on their backs
Just like fish drugged by expert fishermen in the ponds
Or they flap like little fishes out of water: unable to breathe.

*   *   *

The smoke from cigarettes has engulfed the room
It is the strong smoke from native tobacco mixed with cigarettes'
Added to the tallow smoke from candles on the wall
The thick eddy would resemble moving clouds.

14

Add to it the heat from drunk beer oozing out as sweat
And the carbon dioxide breathed out by so many people
And the smell of broken wind and unbrushed or rotten teeth
And the morning dew, and urine of careless men
Louts who cannot control themselves but let urine out
In public, flowing down their trousers:
The air in the room would be thick, thick like iron.

*   *   *

In the urinal place the air is ammoniacly thick
The ground is wet, and men splash about.
And you'd hurry out, or choke! cursing "Goddamn!"
You'll meet with pressed drunks hurrying past
Who would already be unzipping before reaching the urinal
Already dazed, they would urinate as they went;
These are would-be important men, fully bearded, and worthy
        of respect
Having difficulties releasing their urine as if syphilis-hit!

*   *   *

The smell from the latrine hits you from afar
And when you get in, it is as if you're inside the ogre!
It will knock you flat, like the rhino with its horn
The stench of jayce and dung move up in vapours!

The floor is covered with patches of dung;
All tribes of dung are represented here
The dry ones and those just splashed
The hard old ones and those still steaming hot
There are those long and thin, now rolled up,
And those which huddle in mini-heaps!

Vomit and urine flow together
The used anuses are rubbed on the walls
The marks made are red, blood red like ochre
Or dark, extremely dark and smooth, like clay

15

And the wall is criss-crossed with foolish graffiti.
Ochol stop looking down on African culture
Stop jumping about, and foolishly despising .
Stop behaving like the tiny and foolish beer fly
Making much noise over what is not his.
If we decided to hit you back with abuses
And criticisms of the European ways you now ape
Would you stand it? A fully grown-up man
A youth looking for marriage, master upholder of the
     best of his culture
Don't you go far into the bush to answer nature's call?
Isn't it only cowards who defecate indoors or near home?

    *   *   *

It is true, my husband, foreigners' dances I do not know,
Besides, their games too I do not know;
Holding one's partner tightly, in public, I cannot bring
     myself to do;
The dances of foreigners I do not despise.
To me they look like preludes to immoral acts
With the girl demanding the bride price for herself instead
     of her father;

To me, the rumba is a detestable dance
However hard you try to force me to dance it you will fail.
For it is a dance without the accompanying songs
It is a dance danced in silence, as if people were witches
It is a dance without respect, danced when people are drunk:
Fathers and mothers are variously embraced without respect.

And when somebody insists on coercing me to dance the rumba
I would prefer to hang myself, upside down;
I fear I may not hold my tongue, and blurt out a shameful abuse.
Could I become the killer lightning, I know where I would hit!

16

My husband does not want to recall our youth when he was captivated by my beauty. (He does not know Acholi youth dances!)

·When I was young I was the chief of women:
For I was bright, quick and alert;
I was not clumsy, I was scrupulous;
I was healthy, I was slim;
I wasn't broody, I wasn't slow.
I did not grow up uncultured;
I am not shy and will tell you off.
My body was plump, the skin shiny.
When I moved, the earth shook.

At the time Ochol was still wooing me
My breasts stood at ninety degrees;
I walked like the crane: neck up in the air
My brothers were full of praise, calling me Bringer-of-Cows
For, the rhythm of my breasts beckoned bride-wealth:

> Prepare the kraal
> Prepare the kraal
> The cows are coming.

I was the leader of our girls.
Which girl in my in-laws' home was equal to me?
My name was the rage of all Payira;
I played the lyre well, praising my lover.

*   .*   *

17

My friend Ochol, why do you withhold the truth?
You know you knew me when I was in my prime.
In pursuit of me you used to shed bitter tears.
Didn't you spend sleepless nights because of youthful me?

When I was young you admired my lace
Nicely wrought in the Acholi fashion;
The inner roof of our house was well-made with reed
My father built it with Acholi skill;
You had a look at my sister's waist-beads
That my mother had patterned in the best Acholi ways;
You used to shake all over when you saw the tattoos
On my chest and waist and the gap in my teeth.

Truly speaking my man, you are merely talking
For you had seen when I was nubile;
Then, at the thought of losing me, you broke into tears;
You used to hang around our home, come rain or beating.

Fellow, you are denying the past for nothing!
Why doesn't the truth shame you sometimes?
Why do you persist in denying what you know?
This husk is a sorry sight to behold, it brings tears to my eyes!
What really is itching my husband, I keep on asking,
Has he a boil, ripe and ready to burst?

You let the whiteman take you in with tea
You behave as if you're drunk on strong *arak,*
Or move listlessly as though famished or drugged!
Look at him stagger and swear he hates his wife
Trying to be proud because of the tie on his neck.
What a shame!

*   *   *

In my youth I was chief of women
For my manners were good and my movement supple,
I sang in various keys while grinding or going to the well!
In the sweetness of voice, richness of tone, who could compet
    with me?

But now Ochol claims that I am inadequate
That I have become the sloughed-off snake skin, of no use:
Simply because I cannot strum the guitar
And because I turn away from the shameful dance;
That because my ears do not want to hear the rumba tunes
Or because I cannot repeat or follow gramophone records
Or because I cannot turn on and tune his radio;
That, besides, I do not know Swahili and Luganda tongues
Ochol now thinks he has a strong case for rejecting me!

My husband gives me no time to state my case
He has closed up all the avenues for my appeal
He has closed up his own mind, mindlessly;
Now he shouts senselessly like drunken old men
Saying he rejects the wife who has a gap
He now prefers his beauty a woman full of teeth
Whose teeth fill up her mouth like a foreign thing
Who resembles slaves, famine-brought
Wild-featured, unkempt hair! What a beast!

*   *   *

Take it easy my man, don't be too hasty;
Don't close your future ways by undue reactions.
For, know this: the hyena's fashion
Differs from the leopard's; the latter is a marvel!

Take it easy, my friend, go slow,
Your people's prayers will always steady your steps.

Don't behave as if you are shielded by a rock;
Know this: you grew up nourished by African milk.

*   *   *

Daily, you run after European culture
Daily, you run after foreign ways,
Don't you have Acholi ways to keep you going?
Don't the Acholi also have a culture of their own?
You stampede headlong for the whiteman's games
You turn here and there enamoured by foreign arts.
Does the *lawala* not teach sportmanship enough?
From time immemorial didn't your people have
     games of their own?

You leave your own, and head towards foreigner's dances;
You flop and flap, staggering to the whiteman's music
As if you did not have dances of your own!
As if you did not have a lyre of your own! Oh, dear!

It is ignorance that is killing you: you are poor at native dances!
It is shame that is deterring you: you don't know our dances!
It is fear that is keeping you: you're clumsy in our dances!
It is weakness that is stopping you from your people's vigorous
     dances!
It is lack of skill that is hurting you; you can't sing properly!
Are you man enough to start a song in the dancing arena?
You're inept at playing the gourd percussion, or responding
     in the chorus!
Can you rub music from the calabash back? Can you shake the
castanets?

You complain too much, most of it lacks substance:
It is all froth and wind, all truths by half.
If you are a truly cultured man, how many songs do you know?
Stop jumping from topic to topic. Answer me.

How many *bwola* songs have you danced?
Tell me, since you talk so much!
The beating of the *bwola* drum, can you do it?
Tell me truly Ochol, since you call yourself a champion!
Yes, admit it! The mere decorating of the calabash, have
     you done it?

Why have you covered yourself up completely?
Do you have calluses on your hip to hide?
Get up, disrobe, and go to dance the *otole* dance!
Or what is the scar our man is covering from view?

Stop your abuses, my man, or I shall answer you back.
Are there boils protruding atop your buttocks?
What is it you are covering on your hips?
We have to get to the bottom of Ochol's complexes yet!

Ochol is merely inadequate, he is inept in Acholi ways
That is why he fully immerses himself in foreigner's ways:
It is shame and inferiority complex that is hurting my man:
Inverse inferiority complex forces him to grab foreign ways.

*   *   *

You are a failure in life, you float without a base
You wander from place to place as if you have no home,
You have no voice, you have become a middle-man:
You convey the words of another man, as if you're no
     man yourself;
You have become a loud-speaker, you shout like a parrot,
Where's the garden you call your own? Depender on
     handed-down things!
When owners of well-tilled gardens are reaping, you carry
     their harvest for them!
My husband has become a beast of burden, indeed!

21

Don't you sense the people's laughter and derision?
Don't you hear foreigners' challenges and criticisms?
They are alleging that Blacks are filled with venereal diseases.
They are despising us. And don't you stir up? You don't
    answer back?
Listen, Brother! Pumpkin boles in an abandoned homestead
    you do not uproot!

My husband despises traditional African dresses and hair-styles and loves the artificial hair of his modern wife

The man despises me that I don't know modern ways,
That I still dress my hair in the olden styles
That I am timid, bashful and also backward
That my hair is not modernly done and I am not well turned out.

It is impossible for me to dress my hair like a European!
Bear this in mind: my father is from Payira
My mother is native-born; Koch people are my uncles:
I am a pure Acholi not half this half that.
Besides I was not bought by money nor a captive of war;
My mother herself was not purchased with grains.
Besides, my father was not a bought slave.
In the ways of the Acholi, there's nothing I don't know.

My mother's people are in Koch Goma
She taught me all the hair-styles of the Acholi
And when I dressed my hair that way, all boys turned their heads.
Whenever I made my appearance, to tell you the truth
All the boys stopped and stared at me:
My mother did teach me all fashions
That fit the African hair.

As ostrich feathers differ from those of chicken
And the monkey's tail differs from that of the otter;
As the eggshells of alligators differ from those of partridges

The clumsy hippo pads her way naked to the sea;
And Indian hair resembles the tail hairs of camels
It looks like sisal strands and dèserves trimming,
It is shiny black, but also differs from the whiteman's.

European hair is different; it is soft and thin
It feels like silk, or like the hair of colobus monkey,
It is tawny, light and soft to touch
It resembles the monkey's, and differs from mine.

African hair is different; it is crinkly and massed
It forms a rug on one's head, it is not wavy.
At times ringworm clears parts of it, leaving patches
That would embarrass a lady; it is a headache.
But there's a cure; plaster it with porridge
Under the kigelia tree, dancing to this tune:
Omemelo that licked up Oduka's hair
Here's your porridge, feed on it!

Soon after, her hair would be back, she'd be glad.

Acholi hair is carded to satisfaction
With the long wooden comb that straightens the crinkles. .
Nubian women plait their hair instead
It is twined and ends in braids.
But African hair is never left to grow haywire
Only wizards leave their hair to grow anyhow!
Wild men from East Acholi and menstrual women
Leave their hair to grow hirsute and are frightful to behold;

Their chins are covered with manes like lions'
They resemble the bearded billy-goat
Their faces would be covered up in hair.
Neither do they use the warm ash to pluck away
The pubic hair as is the fashion of the sane.
They do not use the tweezers to pinch out beards

And their armpits are left to grow wild
Issuing forth scents that are brine and beastly.
Their general appearance is frightening: dark eyes
Dirty rotten teeth, and emaciated behinds.

In our culture mourning women, or those wearing weeds
Abandon their hair to grow unattended, their pride is gone,
They strip all signs of pride or happiness, including jewels,
For they are bemoaning the tragic life that man lives.

I know all manner of hair-styles
That suit the different states we are in:
Hair-styles for dances, or for outings are different
When one is bereaved, there's no need to dress well.
Mothers who have just delivered have their heads cleanly shaved.

*   *   *

Ochol is setting me aside because he says I love dirt
That I love to heap dirt on my head
That my use of cane-rat's fat makes my head itch.

He claims that African traditional ways are for old people
That they belong to the past, and he's a modern man.
That my mere touching of his clothes dirties them
I can't sleep with him for I'd dirty his sheets,
He claims that I look bad when attired the native way.
My husband shuns me as if I have yaws
He treats me as if I have a communicable disease

When I go past him, he would click and give me dirty looks:
He has now sworn never to touch my hand!

My husband prefers Clem the long-haired one!
She's that standard beauty now, especially since she has been
to school too!
Ochol pines all day long for his darling Clementine
Thoughts about her keep the young man awake all night!

25

My rival, when she's back from roasting her hair
You'd think it was a chick pulled out from a pond.
The hair would shine like twisted python, it is smelly too!
My rival would resemble a cock that's daily pecked!

The hair is burnt with a hot iron
Then it is heat-dried to make it long
It is then rolled around iron wheels, and looks ghastly
Like dog's vomit! That's it: the new beauty for you!

The heat turns the hair brownish
Then plenty of oil is used on it; it smells so!
Then, to make it dark-looking, black shoe-polish is used
To reproduce the natural blackness, to mask the early grey hair
Different dyes are used to mask greying hairs.
The deception does not affect the root-hairs though, they still
        tell tales
And the discrepancy makes you pity the poor woman.

Water does not touch their heads
Smells from damp dandruff follow them everywhere
Sometimes this rubbish heap is bound with a scarf
The smell however comes through, it defies covering up.

At times Clem makes her hair into heaps
Then she resembles a true potato garden
That has been raided by beasts; it looks like a salt-lick
Like a river bank, with turf here and there.
Baldness is the preserve of men
Like beard and side-burns
Baldness is unbecoming in women!
When a woman's head is bald, she looks piteous!

Daily use of the brush has left her head hairless
The brush has swept her hair away up to the middle
The bald front shines bright when the sun is up

Poor girl, she now combs her hair front-ward:
It still shines through when lightning flashes.

Sometimes she wears dead people's hair
The hair of a white woman who died long ago
After donning it she goes boldly to dance!
Meanwhile, the real owner disintegrates, buried long ago!
What type of witchcraft is this my people?

If mother luck is not with you, the wig falls off
Then the shame is great! Oh, my people!
If such happened to me, I would break down and cry!

When Ochol enthuses over his Clementine
He despises me, he degrades all I know
He prides himself because of Kele, the whore
Who ties up her head, covering hyena hair
The scarf is in place to cover the stuff
The scarf is in place to cover bald head.
The ugly-so, instead of returning to her home
Has now stuck on my husband like a magnet!
Or like lice that feed parasitically on dogs.

*   *   *

The head of the spirit-child has a tuft left in the middle;
Otole-dancers smear red-ochre, and dance in line
They look orderly, pleasing to the heart!
Young girls growing up to attract husbands
Whose breasts are still breaking out small-small,
Smear themselves all over with the sesame oil
They wear one or two elephant tail necklaces!
They use shea-butter, collected from Got Ajulu,
Oil that comes from Labwor-omor.
They are healthy, fast and active.
They are smooth and well-fed, cheeks not sunk in.

. ne ghec that has been churned .
Leaves one's skin completely smooth;
The fat from edible rats, the big or small ones
When brewed with sweet-smelling and long-smelling herbs
You use it today the smell remains till tomorrow,
You'll still be clean, and the skin soft and shiny.
You'll be attractive, your suitors would demand
  another appointment
When boys chance on you, they'd like to propose!

Under such conditions, when you go the well
You wouldn't come back in a hurry!
When the pot you're carrying matches your beauty
Prospective suitors ask whose daughter you are!

Ochol my friend, I am a pure Acholi
My hair is the true Black man's hair.
Don't absorb all foreign propaganda
That all African things are bad.

I do not intend to resemble aliens
There's no reason why I should use foreigners' cultures
Heaping hair like a witch, like a killer,
Like a possessed person, where is the beauty there?

Asking people to mend their ways does not break the bond!
What is spoiling Clementine is her desire to ape white women.
Why don't you tell her off? She's your wife, you've the power
To stop her from heaping her hair anyhow
Baldness is unseemly when seen on a woman's head
Ochol my man, try to rescue my rival, I beg you!
Please try: talk to the Bull's daughter.

How come no whites have taken to African ways?
You are the only ones who have deserted ancestral ways
You give out that you're educated and know a lot
Then you go white-aping, causing us such an anguish!

I have pride in my black skin:
The very one with which I was born;
I have pride in the colour of my skin
With which my mother bore me!
I am not ashamed because of the hair
With which my mother bore me!
Which leopard wishes to change places with the hyena?
Which crested crane craves the baldness of the
    offal-eating vulture?
Which elegant giraffe wishes to change and become a wolf?
Which multi-coloured butterfly wants to become a dung-beetle?

One's ancestral heritage cannot be deserted.

My husband rejects me because I hate
European foods, cookery and table manners.
(But each culture determines what is eaten,
on what it is served and how it is cooked!)

My husband hates me because I don't know European foods
That I am unskilled in eating with spoons
That I can't hold the eating utensils well
And that I do not know how to look after a house well.

He says I don't know the foods the moderns eat:
Besides I do not know how to cook the European way
He complains that I don't like to gobble up chicken
Or feast on the slimy half-cooked eggs!
He says I am a fool, for, why should I get sick
Whenever he brings me tins of crabs and frogs?
Sometimes he slaps me hard
Because I prefer calabash to chinaware.

He continuously harps at my lack of school education
Claiming it's the cause of my ignorance of modern cooking:
My inability to cook with the stove, how to light it
Ochol attributes all these to my lack of school education.

I do admit without shame that
Cooking the European way is foreign to me
Using charcoal for cooking I don't know
The thought of it takes my desire for cooking away.

Whoever said charcoal was for cooking?
Perhaps it is appropriate for cooking jackals
And all sorts of beasts women don't eat!

The power of *elektik* light kills people;
For that is a portion of lightning power;
If you touch it, it will race all the way to your heart!
To use *elektik* for cooking is no easy thing.
The bullet from the sky – who has ever touched it?
The sky dwelling red-cock has now become a cooking fuel!
The red-cock has truly become a torch for lighting streets!
It frightens me, I keep away from it.

Brother, this cooking hearth is difficult to use
Who has ever done her cooking whilst standing up?
This stove can't cook green vegetables well.
How to underprop a pot on its flat surface is tough!
There's even nowhere for putting the large pot for
        stirring porridge!
The whole hearth is as flat as a house-floor
How is one supposed to cook on it?
I rake my mind figuring out how to use it till I tire
Besides, there are so many buttons to push!

European cooking tops are made for cooking European foods
For making meat look like it is cooked;
It is good for half-frying chicken eggs
Which run in the plate like phlegm, smell like a skunk.
The flat top is suitable for cooking with the flat pans
Or other European cooking utensils whose bottoms are flat;
All these flat European fire-tops dishearten me
For none of them suits my purpose
For, satisfactory Acholi cooking needs a pot
Or a saucepan with deepened bottom.

31

Different people make their hearths according to the foods
    they cook
The European stove has a room for baking bread
Its top is suitable for boiling cabbages and other rubbishy foods
It may even do for boiling the Baganda plantains!

Just think: if you have a digging party to feed
And the fatted billy-goat is slaughtered
And the millet flour is full in the sack
And shelled cow-peas fill half a sack
When fifteen gourds are filled with milk
And three huge pots are full of beer ......
Will charcoal stoves or paraffin stoves do the job?
Can the *elektik* fire on the flat surface do the trick?

    *   *   *

The right woods for special cooking are *opok* or shea
We bring home bundles of *oduggu* and *ogali*
And with these we simmer the hippo-hide biltong overnight:
If you don't cook it well people will boo you.

Cooking with stoves defeats me completely:
It is only bachelors who use charcoal stoves.

Cooking with the stove I detest:
When the stove buzzes as it cooks, I am frightened,
As with all European machines, it makes noise
And when it explodes, especially in the dry season
The fire would destroy a ridge and a half.

Using the stove for cooking is tough
To begin with, I don't know how to light it.
And, it does not permit me to wiggle the paste into the sauce.
When it is blocked, I can't find the hole to pierce;
And the odour of paraffin and my head don't agree.
Finally, to put it off, I don't know how.

Charcoal and paraffin stoves are hateful to me
They both can hardly knead the millet bread
To cook the millet bread you need to have live flames
To wrap up the pot and cook all sides well.
For the dances that last the whole night
Our youth should have something solid inside them:
Something tough, warm, and well-turned.
When the bread is soft the boys will jeer;
Or they'll slap their sisters hard for poor cooking.

The stove is not suited for cooking your man's midnight treat
Or for drying the meat of a big game carcass
That is caught in a noose, or deep hole: it will go to waste.
The paraffin stove meets the indiscriminate needs of bachelors.

Ochol, our forests still teem with wood
Besides making and using our hearth is easy.
Don't drain my strength wrestling with stoves.
My friend, if you quiz me on types of wood
The right wood for cooking fuel, and all their names
I can tell them to you one by one and you'll be amazed.
For I know them by their leaves and fruits:
The *oywelo* and *kituba* and *lucoro* are no good for fuel:
They are powdery and do not produce a flame,
They are equal to papaya whose fire is also weak
They can't even be used for roasting locusts.

The *labwori* wood is good only when dry
If there is still dampness left
It produces enough smoke to drive away unwanted guests
Or men who stick by their wives in the cooking place!
The smoke from the labwori wood is good for chasing
       Odure away
These are men who guard their wives as they cook

Suspecting them of eating the better portion of meat as
    they cooked.
These are weak people who sustain themselves by snatching foods.

    Odure, take your leave
    Leave the fire place alone
    Lest flying sparks scorch your crotch!

The log from the *opok* tree sunders easily;
The shea-butter tree burns slowly, nicely
Poi the iron-tree is not wood, it is a hard rock
Its wound turns septic; it is only good for old-age walking staff.

*   *   *

Brother, cooking with European stoves messes me up:
But I know our types of firewood from the first to the last:
Those a snake has crawled on break into sparks
They also itch the body that has rubbed against them.

When our women are heavy with child
Never do they step across burning logs
For lightning would hit them; the pestle is also a taboo to them:
They do not walk over it, they go a-skirt it.

The leaves of the *obuga* are cooked thick and matted
But the leaves of peas and lady-fingers float in the watery sauce;
Our cooking place is dug, it is sunk into the floor
But that of my uncles' people is built up, three-legged!
All Acholi hearths are for round-bottomed tapering pots.
The flat-bottomed aluminium pan
Suffices for boiling tea or Gulu town cooking types
But for the real African cooking, the saucepan will let you down.

Atop the pressure-stove the earthen pot cannot sit
And when the millet-bread has to be turned
If one has no rag to hold the pot up
You're in trouble: it will exhaust you completely.

This is a taste of the life bachelors lead in workplaces
When they live alone making do with charcoal and
    pressure stoves
They burn while cooking, looking for the dowry wealth
That's why when they return home, they hurry to marry
These contract labourers, when they're back home
They rush to marriage like eager drinkers of beer
Cooking with stoves had made their plight worse!

   *   *   *

Our age-old plates are the half-gourds
Our sauce is dished out into the earthen *atabo*;
The aluminium dish looks white and nice
But it also suffers from dirt.
I have no desire to use foreigners' utensils:
The aluminium plate lets you down when you want
    to keep it clean!

It changes colour, becomes grey or lacklustre
When you scour it, because it is not plated, the
    aluminium washes off.
After two or three serious washings, there's a hole
Which, when not gummed in time,
Might one day let all your soup flow away leaving
    the bread untouched.

The native earthenware, glazed, red and shiny
Especially after it has absorbed oil from repeated use
When it is broken it should be replaced.
If it was broken on purpose, it may provoke or deepen a feud.
The earthenware serving dishes are good: they keep foods warm.
They do not let heat flow away like aluminium plates.

The thick and heavy sauce of lentils
The special dish of people of Koch - my in-laws! -
Loved by their Chief Lagony, should be eaten warm.

Even the fresh hibiscus leaves cooked without paste
But infused with a good measure of hot pepper
If it is to refresh one, to let the blood flow once more,
It should be eaten warm, not ice-cold.

The fatted sternum or the hump of the zebu bull
Is not edible when it has become cold
And is covered with thick layer of fat fly-studded.

The *malakwang* sauce that has received a generous sesame paste
And is infused with tomato paste, is eaten in mouthfuls;
Sometimes it may be cooked with the hippo hide or skin lining
     oxen eyes
Thrown in to blunt its harshness, is scooped with the potato
But it must be warm to taste good;
If it had gone cold, it is best that it be warmed.
A woman's favourite calabash for bread which
May be white inside, or decorated on the outside
Is best: it does not let bread sweat, wetting it all over;
It keeps the heat in, and the bread remains fresh and warm.

Porridge is best served in the natural calabash
To give you that satisfaction that pleases,
Its warmth infuses into one, making sweat break out.
But served in a plate and drunk with a spoon? This is no
     porridge at all!

Besides, the aluminium cup and plate
With hot porridge in it is hot like fire;
The aluminium cup is okay for tea or *arak*;
If you served the tamarind-mixed porridge in it
Or the porridge-to-become-beer, and when these have cooled
And heavy components sunk to the bottom
Even if you throw in pints of honey
Nothing will happen: the aluminium has killed the
     fermentation process.

When I come home from weeding after sundown
Or when I am back home after collecting fire-wood
Do not bring me water in a glass, however clean.

Whenever I am sated with beans or ants
Or even the thick sauce made of sesame paste;
When the *omel* fish or *chamtunu* is cooked
Or the Nile-perch or whichever fish
Including the small *lakalachede* or the mammoth cow-size turtle
Bring me water in a large calabash
So that I may drink and feel superb.

When a woman has just delivered
Water doled out in small glasses increases her thirst
It does not hit thirst-bottom; it evaporates on the way.

*   *   *

We eat our meals sitting down
For we have no tables for eating on
Eating whilst one is perched atop a tree like apes.
In our house even if you had desired it,
You'd not succeed; for my father's ritual stool
Is the only wooden chair around.
All the rest of us, children and our mothers
Sit down on skins or carpets
Girls sit with their ankles neatly bent beneath them,
Boys sit crossing legs, all quiet and respectful.

The table knife in our custom is used for shredding greens
Or harvesting grains, cutting up meats or offals in bits;
Or toothless people use it to reduce meat into swallowable bits!
But the knife is never used for cutting up millet bread.
Our children wash clean their hands
And then use them to scoop up millet bread
And eat it till their stomachs are full.

In my father's house even the left-handers
Have to use their right hands for scooping bread
Only those who have no respect use their left hands:
And these are worthless people who would come to sorry ends.
Their action shows poor up-bringing and lack of self-respect.
This etiquette is known Africa-wide!

I have no liking for raking food with a fork:
Why do you fork it up, is it bitter?
Ochol carries food to his mouth in a forked instrument:
Has food become a serpent, do you carry it like that because
     it is bad?

Ochol my man, however much you ape the whiteman
Even if you're acquainted with the whiteman's teaching
Stop calling people fools, as if you were a whiteman!
However much you strive to eat like a whiteman
Do not forget that you are not a whiteman.
Please remember the African proverb:
The ancient pumpkin in the old homestead is never uprooted.
Indeed Ochol, you are a blackman.
Who has ever uprooted the cultural pillars of his people?

My husband rejects me because I do not know how to reckon or keep European time

My man shuns me because he says I am poor at keeping time.
He says I don't even know how to count the years
Or the name of the month when our first son was born.

He quizzes me "How many days are in a year?"
And: "How many Sundays in four months?"
But I am at a loss to answer these:
"How many moons in nine Sundays?"
I don't know!

Ochol has mounted the biggest clock on our wall,
It goes sek-sek-sek-sek- and rings a bell.
There's a lot of twisting before it starts to move
This is an action I have never brought myself to do.
When I hear its rhythm I am all in wonder;
And when I see the arms move I hold my mouth.
And all around its rim there are numbers written;
It has a long testicle, loosely suspended on a string.

Telling time by the clock defeats me
For I am still ignorant of figures and arithmetic;
Left to me, I regard it as a decoration on the wall:
It looks beautiful, it impresses guests, makes me proud.

Telling time by Ochol's clock is a mystery
It doesn't make sense: when it's early morning they say it's eight!
And when the cocks crow they say it is eleven!
And when the sun sets they say it is seven!

39

This type of telling time turns my head round and round.
All is upside down: what was down is now regarded up,
Like a children's game where you run round and round till
    you're utterly confused.

*   *   *

Ochol my husband, as to the time of your waking up
Or for boiling tea and serving cold breakfast,
Time for drinking coffee and taking photographs;
Time for breakfast and midday meal
Or time for your supper at night
I first look at the sun and ascertain from there,
The cocks have first to crow to set me going.

In my culture if one has a long journey to go
Or there's a hunt or communal work to tackle, it is at dawn
That one sets out: at morning glow; not midnight pitch.
Early activities begin after first cock-crows
When the morning star rules the Eastern sky like another moon.
Only wizards move at night, when it is darkest, bewitching
    people;
And maybe fornicators returning home from midnight intrigues.

Night is time for rest and sleep
When tiny babies snuggle close to their mothers' chests
It is only young men hot with romance
Who are out; hurrying back home at the crow of cocks!
They would hurry home, playing hide and seek with ghosts
Which are on the loose, spreading chicken or small pox!
Illicit sex is sweeter than the sweetest fruits:
The romancers defy nocturnal dew and mosquito bites.

When the sun has climbed up
And its barbs are now sharp like arrows
Biting hard at backs of diggers and harvesting or weeding girls
Then the housewife takes drinking water
To the people who have been digging since cock-crow.

Food will be taken when the workers are tired
Then the relief team takes over the hoes
Whilst the cultivators eat and drink:
They'd leave behind a large new garden.
And flies would settle on what is left.

In the evening when the sun has lost its fiercer barbs
Men and boys check on their traps,
They hunt the bush-rat, carve a dish
They twine tethers for cows, or make chicken coops;
They repair granary roofs, or decorate some gourds;
Some make yarns to entangle star-eyed girls.
The herdsboys return home blowing their flutes and horns,
They are bringing wealth home:
The bulls would low, and their owners would praise them!
The goat herds would light the courtyard fire.

*   *   *

The blessed woman has produced a dutiful daughter
Who does all the work, whilst her mother sits and relaxes.

But if your daughter is a play-girl
With whom men have sex, even in the bush
Then her reputation is gone, she is light and cheap.

You'll work yourself to death, as if you have no child!
To the woods, to the grinding rock you'll go: a woman of
        no respect!
You'll break your back cooking whilst your daughter is
        out romancing!
You'll break your back taking bath water for your man
And wish you had never hatched this freak.
Expert musicians would compose a song detailing your position:

    This girl's mother wastes away grinding flour
    As if she never bore a daughter

41

Her daughter is big and lazy, what to do?
The good mother wears herself out carrying water
Her daughter has no shame or consideration
Her daughter is big and lazy, what to do?

The dutiful daughter of the blind dame
Plays with others but is conscious of domestic duties.
The daughter who has mastered all household chores
Frees her mother from cooking the evening meal
The mother is only called to come and dish out,
It is only after the house is cleaned, beddings spread,
That boys and good girls go out to dance
Leaving their aged parents to reminisce at home.

*   *   *

Ochol says I am wasteful, I waste time
He insists that I am incapable of keeping time
That I am totally unconscious of time
And therefore he has no time
To waste on me.

He does not want to pass time chatting gaily
Inexpert he is in joking repartees, neither does he frequent
    the evening courts
He sits lonely, mouth tightly shut
And growls should noise reach his ears.
Now, does the noise innocent children make hurt your ears?
Would you rather we had no children and were quiet?
Deadly quiet so you can read your papers in peace?
Isn't it by bearing more children that a home increases?

At the shrine, don't elders entreat that more children be born?
Don't they pray that the blessing of child-bearing should
    descend on women?

42

In the dance arena where women dance the *ogodo*
Isn't it the mother of many, the lucky woman
Who dances best, lifting high her neck?

*   *   *

Whenever Ochol is engrossed in reading a new book
Should a child cough, you'd hear "Goddamn!"
And he'd hurl a fire-brand in that direction.

When he relaxes in his easy chair
And has enveloped himself with large dailies
He'd look like a shroud! He's in an evil mood
Has turned anti-man, and is lonely, like the tomb!

My husband has made time his Chief
Ochol has become time's prisoner-in-chief:
He's always on the run, obeying his chief.

Whenever visitors arrive his mien begins to darken
He'd greet them up-standing and demand: "What can I do
     for you?"
Two selfishnesses have met: his inborn and this derived one!
When he shuts himself up in his office, his mouth would be
     tightly closed!
When I come up on matters of domestic urgency he chases
     me away
Insisting that he has no time, and should not be disturbed!

*   *   *

I freely admit: keeping European time I do not know
I am adept at keeping Acholi times: my mother taught these
     to me
It is therefore uncouth of people to shout new demands at me!
For I am practising the Acholi ways that I know.
The right time for suckling a child
For putting him to bed and waking him up

43

His time for playing and for a bath
The time when a child crawls and when he starts to toddle
The time for weaning a child and giving him food
The age a child begins to talk
Reckoned in the European's way I don't know: I am Acholi
My mother brought me up the Acholi way.

When a child cries, give it the breast
For crying is its way of showing hunger.
When a child cries, clinging on to you
Maybe it is sick, has intestinal disturbance!

The first aid for a sick child is the breast!
When you give it milk, it will shut up.
Even if it is sick, keep it suckling
Meanwhile send someone to call the medicine man.

Children in our land do not sleep according to time
When sleep overpowers a child, it will sleep;
When sleep is finished it will wake up.
Sometimes when children cry it is a prelude
That's a sign sleep is approaching, let them suckle
Because, as they cry, sleep comes;
When a child cries, running to you
Give it milk, straightaway it will sleep.

Whenever a child's body is covered with dirt, wash it
You don't have to wait till the time demarcated;
If there is no bath water, let it wait.
But after you have bathed it clean
Rub its body all over with sesame oil
Or grease its body with the curative shea-butter.
When you leave a child unlotioned like a beast
When you don't care for its skin
Or you do not oil its body enough, then all over
The skin would crack up, particularly in the dry season.

And, in the cold season it would suffer from cold.
Besides, any sickness would get worse; the child would get weak.

*   *   *

Listen to me, Ochol, in the Acholi traditions
Time is not chopped up in tiny bits
Called *sekonda* and *dakika*. Besides, it does not flow
Like lachoi beer through a straw.
Time does not drip away like the lye salt
And then dry up when the water is gone
Only to be cast away into the rubbish bin.
Period is not like our millet meal
Around which hungry hunters sit!
It does not finish like sauce in a plate
Neither does it resemble the shade which, when lost,
      death follows!
It does not go bad like the rotting buck the hunters
      have forgotten.

The Acholi hate idlers and indolent people
In cookery, in harvest-time or in digging-time
The Acholi want the end result to show: enough food produced.
It is not slavishly sticking to time they're after.
Whipping is the fate of those who hide when there's work, ·
Or who malinger, saying they're sick, but would get up quick
      to eat:
If there is no food what would happen when visitors come?
When they spend the night hungry, won't they go and tell tales?

It is a well-known fact that when there's famine
Women go abroad to buy or work for food
And become easy game for lecherous men with sellable grain
They would exchange grain for sex.

*   *   *

Ochol laughs at me quizzing: "What are the names of
    the months?"
He teases me further with: "How many months are in a year?"
He continues his laughter with: "How many Sundays are in
    a month?"
As far as I know Sundays are prayer days for the new believers!
It is their day for shouting non-stop, a head-ache day
To both Catholic and Protestant believers.

There's no day set aside for worshipping Acholi Gods:
If an epidemic or calamity has hit a home
The eldest woman makes travelling provisions ready
Sends an emissary to call home all the extended family
And a communal gathering is held round the ancestral shrine.

When war has broken out or a communal hunt
The Chief pacifies the clan spirits,
If it was the dry season, a goat would be speared
In the grazing ground, and blessings would be sought;
Auguries would be read from the intestines, divinations
    by sandals
And the departed ancestors are asked to bless hunters' lives!

As for the moon, we all know it very well!
It comes out as a new moon, climbs up, then goes down;
It lightens night-time making it become clear;
When the moon is full, one urges one's mother-in-law to depart;
Evil-hearted men hate bright moon indeed
Even the hyena cries out that the bright moon hurts his eyes.

The moon is seen by all women
It is a clear indicator that a girl has puberty attained
And that should she have sex she'd conceive
Unless she happens to be non-productive.

Refusing to have sex with your man is tabooed:
It is forbidden from one end of Africa to the other
But no sex is allowed when baby has not yet teethed
All this time the child is a half-formed thing and should mature
That baby should not have a sibling born yet;
No sex is allowed when a woman is menstruating
It is advisable for her to turn away from her man
Lest desire overpowers her and she breaks a taboo.

Pregnancy whilst one is suckling changes the quality of milk:
The baby would be weak, not crawl in time, with a tummy big
Weak spindly legs: it would not walk.
Eating is all it knows, like baby locusts, day and night.

Normal pregnancy lasts eight full moons
By then the child is ready to come out.
But should a child come out before this
It is called *abwoga,* meaning 'premature'.

*　　　　*　　　　*

I admit I do not know the names of the months
For the Acholi have no names for them.
We know the season for dry sowing,
We call that period *Ager*
When you stir up much dust as you plough.
The rains fall in the *Poto-kot,* meaning "falling rains"
And cause the planted seeds to sprout.
Sometimes this season comes early, at others late.
When the millet has started to bear grains
Each farmer begins to make plans for storage
For, harvest-time is soon to follow:
That period is called *Odunge* - meaning "expectations".

When some fingers of millet have started to ripen
Hasty men, or those with no reserve, will not wait
For they are tired of drinking green-leaves sauce without bread

47

Should you raise your brow, they would demand: "Whose
    garden is it, anyway?"
They cut ripe heads of grain from place to place.
This season is called *Abalo-pa-nga*?
Meaning: Whose garden have I spoilt?

*   *   *

In our land we know the rainy and dry seasons:
The rainy season spells garden work:
Sowing, weeding, harvesting: hard and dirty work;
It is no time for malingerers; you come home dusty or muddy,
It entails waking up betimes, brushing through the dewy grass.
The rainy season means exhaustion from beginning of season
    to its end
It shows up the weak, lazy, and those without resolve!

The dry season signifies leisure, means dances
It entails hunting expeditions and camp activities.
The drums would sound for *otole* dance, and others for
    funeral dances;
The horns and trumpets of those who have killed would sound.
The youth would chase game after fire has razed their parks,
Lone expert hunters would go away for days
They would dry up buffalo, buck, beeste meat over fire.
Some young men would go to Pajule to search for bride wealth:
Especially those who have no sisters to bring home dowries.
If they kill elephants and sell their teeth
They'd marry and name their first kids "Ocan"
Whose meaning is that they are poor, did not inherit wealth.

In the chase where game is enclosed in a ring of fire
The elephant burns and sprays some water from its trunk
    to cool itself;
The hunters come after the fire keeping the game encircled,
When a wild beast has broken through, expert hunters take
    to their heels!

48

In this hunt, you rest and proceed: "*Itongo ten!*" means stop
    and rest;
The circle is still large, you need some rest
You recover your strength, repair sandals, remove thorns;
When "*Iboole!*" is pronounced, you proceed, closing in on
    the game.

The dry season means romance, means running away with
    a lover;
The *otole* dance is moved to other clans: those with nubile girls,
It is the privilege of Chiefs to invite people to *bwola* dance;
But the wedding dance is danced all night long.

Some evenings under the bright moon
You'll hear girls' voices as they ululate the aria
Atop a hillock, when they number ten or more.

They'd be praising their lovers with seemly songs;
They would direct their barbs at old men who run after girls
Who heap countless presents on their mothers-in-law
These old men who prey on teen-age girls for wives;
They would sing their hearts out, bemoaning their lovers
    who have no cows.

    Rain's bullet hit my husband and kill him
    But please don't hit my lover
    I beg you: spare my lover.

Ochol says my eardrums are full of wax
And that my head is thick, unpenetrated by knowledge!
He claims I am as dumb as the bleating sheep
Because I do not know how to count years.

Brother, I won't tell lies, I accept the charge:
The names of European months I do not know,
And determining time by using European years defeats me;

For, I never stepped into a class-room for a single day
The ways of the whiteman my mother never taught me!

The time when a child was born
We remember by whether it was in the dry or rainy season;
If the sesame-candle light had to be used
Then it was born at night close to the house-post;
We name our children to remember wars, epidemics
And hunts, famines, or locusts that came.

*   *   *

When someone is grown up, it shows:
When she is a girl the breasts will jut out
When he is a boy he will grow his first crop of beard
His voice turns rough, he tires of childish games.

When a girl has attained puberty, is rounded and filled up
She is ready for marriage, prospective husbands begin
        wooing her;
When a boy's testicles hang loosely in the pouch, he is testy;
After three or four deliveries child-birth ceases;
Soon after a girl becomes a woman and she becomes a
        mother-in-law
But if she does not receive the respect she deserves she angers
        quickly
Especially if her daughter is morally loose and unmarried.

Maturity shows through what one does
Through strength of character, through resoluteness
The grown-up man will address an audience with confidence;
The man who is timid or bashful
Is still a child, his spirit is still asleep.

If you are a bachelor, however big you may be
Even if your hair has turned grey all-over,
Or your head is shiny from fallen hair

50

Or your teeth have fallen out because of old age
You are not yet a man: married men call you to eat when it's
    raining.

You are obliged to carry food from kitchen to table
Regardless of how big a physique you may have;
Your ration is with kids; you're still a child!
Whatever achievements you bring, if you are unmarried
Your human development is regarded incomplete
You're never respected; nobody sympathises with you.
Your counterpart in social ostracism is the aged spinster;
The woman who remains unmarried till her breasts have cooled;
A sorry sight when she moves amongst young girls, doing
    their chores!
She helps other women doing their domestic duties
But at night she has no home of her own to go to
For she has no husband at whose house to repair at night.
Her parents bemoan the loss incurred in her up-bringing
And this loss of the expected dowry for another marriage.

        *   *   *

Ochol laughs at me because I can't tell my age
That I have never known the month when I was born
Nor have I known the date on which I was born.

Listen friend, *mwaka* is not a Lwo word:
My brother revealed to me that it is a Swahili word
He told me this at the fire place, where we relax and converse;
He had just returned from the war in Gilgil, a place in Kenya.

Ochol keeps on telling me what does not make sense,
He tells me the story of Jesus, that the time he was born
Long ago in the far away land of Judaya,
That is when the first year started.

He says that before the Mother of Jesus bore him
Years were counted backwards;
That you started with millions of years and kept decreasing them,
You started off with thousands and then reduced them to half
Till it was only hundreds, twenties, tens then one,
When it hit zero-bottom then Jesus was born.
After that you started climbing upwards to one
Then moved on to tens till it reached hundreds five.
And now it has reached a thousand and nine hundred
And sixty-five.

This logic warps up my reasoning, it knots up
My thoughts; I can't figure it out, it leaves me limp.

My husband rejects me because I do not have a Christian name

The son of the bull rejects me for being a *kaffir*
That I don't know the ways of God,
Nor the good words in their new book
Besides, I have not received a new name;
He claims that evil spirits inhabit me
Besides I have not gone through Catechism.
He claims I am addicted to divination like my mum,
Besides, I have not received a Christian name
When I have bouts of spirit possession, he is ashamed
Besides, he hates me because I haven't attained Confirmation.

Ochol despises me because I cannot cross myself properly

> In the Father's name and the Son's
> And the Shade that's Clear - Amen!

He says I cannot receive the Penitence well
I fear some bearded padres with bloated tummies!
He says I don't know the meaning of the Last Oiling.

My husband compares me to the mangy dog
He claims that I have demonic powers!
He talks non-stop, without a pause or awe,
That I am a bloodyfool, a non-Christian.
He asserts that were I a Christian
I would have been a bit better.
But now, even the way to the Church is unknown to me.

*   *   *

53

I had long time ago turned my back against proselytising:
I had refused to be a servant to the wives of other men;
I had refused to be helping maid to a fellow
I had refused to work like a common porter:
Tasks performed merely to purchase a Christian name.

I had refused to break my back heaving water
For teacher's wives, or burn my fingers cooking;
I abhorred extremely slavish treatments:
Like grinding, like digging, like heaving wood
Or smearing a new earthen coat to a wall, like a bride;
Like cutting thatching grass, or grass for catching ants,
Like harvesting, or cutting sesame stalks.
When they're eating you're sent on errands
Or told to go to play, or run about.
For food, we had to depend on gleaned potatoes
As if a major famine had struck the land.
The girls all lost weight and looked pale and wan
Like diarrhoearing cows, with heads like kwashiorkor children.

The Christian name is got after much suffering
You labour and suffer till you are weak:
The wives of priests fatten on free labour.

They regard catechumens as free labourers, apprentices;
While they themselves sit, bask and chat;
In the evening they sit, resting against walls
Waiting only to go and dish out food.

My elder sister received the name Erina.
She - Erina Atoo - read her name from the Protestants.
The amount of suffering she got would make you pity her
Her waist-band could not find her waist any more.

One Sunday I had the urge
To go with her up to her Church,
There we found some man who was very active
He had lifted up his hand, that he was invoking God's blessing
That he was showering luck on his hearers.

There were people kneeling down before his table
Their mouths were wide open like little birds'.

The man officiating did not wear a rosary
He donned a black *kanju* with a white robe on top
In his hand he had a tin plate
Inside it were some broken crumbs, white-looking,
The man's new name was Eliya - a bull name.
He was inviting people to come and eat man-meat.

And they all fell to it with glee!
Then he lifted up a cup filled with human blood!
And they drank it like milk, gullet going up and down!

All these turned my stomach upside down
I realised that man-eating belongs to the Protestant Church!
They're all carnivores and look at you like future meat!
Beware of Protestants, even those who are your kin!

*   *   *

At one time I joined the Catholic's evening classes
But I never remained there long, I ran away!
I ran away from their noisy evening foolishness
Where one shouts like parrots, or crows over refuse.

> Mariya that is clean, mother of God
> Pray for us who are spoilers
> Full of grasya.

All these words never made sense to me
The general shouting as of people possessed;
The Patri shouts senseless, in a foreign tongue;
The Acholi used by Sisters is unintelligible to me
They all shout anyhow, like industrial machines.

One night when the moon was bright
The drums of youth dance were beckoning loudly
The night was clear like very day.
The Catechist was drunk, his eyes red
He went through the process of teaching us Faith
He recited loudly, and we chorused after him
Like weaver birds gleaning in the field.
The teacher shouted in foreign tongues what he did not know
Though he was an Acholi, his voice was rough
He now spoke in Latin like Italian priests.
His nose was blocked, he now spoke through his nose
He would shout on-on-on and we followed suit:
And nobody had any idea what the lesson was all about.

I accept God Patri who is capable over all
The moulder of the sky and the ground ....

The Catechists' name was Bichenchiyo Laguchu
He was drunk, and smiled about, happy with himself.
The drum tune kept coming, loud and clear
We were all stirred up and raring to go!
The song reached us in all its melodiousness,
For it was a joyous dance, a marriage dance.

You'd imagine the happiness of those girls out there
Having a good time with their mates.

Meanwhile Bicheny is shouting like a monkey!
Crying about like a new-born child!
In the dancing arena my song was up!

56

Owin come and let me see you
The daughter of Leng'a-moi, leader of girls
Beloved, return back to me!
Owin the chief of women
Oh, my beloved, let's elope and go
The daughter of Leng'a-moi newly grown
My beloved, come and let me see you
Owin, the chief of women.

Bicheny was deeply involved in conducting prayers:
Your body is lucky amongst women
He was drunk, fierce like powdered acid:
Mariya the Clean One, Mother of God
Beer froth was sputtering from his mouth:
Entreat for us, Spoilers, full of grasya
When he belched, the smell of beer hit you down
He would shout, spraying you with saliva
Belched beer would fill his mouth, he would swallow it back.
And we hurriedly shouted after him, like finches in
     mating season.

The shirt-collar of this teacher was extremely dirty,
Sweat! His cheeks and skin were rough with grown hair
No comb goes through his hair, now overgrown.
His voice was rough, this big black man:
A frightful sight to behold. He looked like a witch
Spoke through his nose, and had a rumbling voice.

*   *   *

Anger came upon me like a shade
I was mad. Had he been my husband
There would have been death, I would have poisoned him!
He was now well-launched, had no idea of an end.
Meanwhile the dance drums beckoned
Others are enjoying life, we are cooped up in class!

In the arena they are praising me
And here I am seated, immobile and dumb.
In the arena my lover is awaiting me
And here I am before this smelly, ugly so and so!

Our patience ran out, we escaped
Racing across the river, past the next ridge
We ran till we broke into the dance arena.
We joined in the chorus of songs we understood,
We danced to death, sweat covered us so!

Let the ugly one waste his time there
A fool who should be whipped to life.
Who had ever tried to keep cattle away from salt-lick?
The time for romance was being wasted in senseless shouts
Whereas life yearned to break out from one's bosom.

At night they would lock you up
When lover's heads should rest on your arms.
You're made to sleep alone like a handleless knife
Whereas even the normal Padre or Soure who is married to
        celibacy
Would be aroused and have sleepless nights!

Now consider the plight of a girl newly grown
Whose breasts are breaking out of her chest
Who is now locked up like a goat
And barred from meeting men and going to dance!

Now! After we had danced a song
Catechist Bicheny broke in!
Drunk, tired, and unable to speak,
With a large percussion calabash he came
To try his luck at wooing girls.
He picked up courage, and said he wanted me,
The old bachelor, started wooing me!

This ugly oldie, started whispering to me!
Shamelessly he even touched my breasts.
I sucked in air, spat on him, and clicked.
He threatened there and then to terminate my course
Saying if I am a fool I would miss the bounties he had!

The bald-headed old man, look at him, don't touch me!
Who is going to die for the sake of a name
You ugly one, shouting senselessly? Leave my arm!
Look at him! Go away! You syphilitic man!
All Catechists are the same:
They're only interested in the breasts of girls
Even the Padres whose oaths forbid them marriage
Sexual desires also disturb them.
Even the very fat ones
Whose fat stomachs hide their navels
When they've fondled a breast they have bliss
Even the Padres in the Penitential booth!

*   *   *

Ochol hates me claiming I've not received my name
He claims my name "Lawino" is not enough;
That Lawino is a useless name, for ignorant people
Hence I have no name that would please his heart.
Ochol would like me to be called Benedeta
He adores the name Achil: Chichilia
He has already named my daughter Marta
One of them carries the heavy name of mother of God: Mariya:

> Mariya who is clean, the Mother of God
> Her body is lucky, it is full of grasya!

He says I am a fool, wasting time on useless things
That I behave like an addling olden fool.
Ochol named his first son Jekchon
His last son is called Parachiko

59

One of his illegitimate sons is called Tomchon,
The other one is called Gulyelmo Iriko.
He insists we should address him with his new name
Even his wives must be called by foreign names.
African names are names of ignorance
He hates superstitions and witchcraft
Ochol strides with pride claiming he's a whiteman now!
He says all African names are heathens' names
They're the names of those who would burn in hell
Because they do not know the Evangeli.
He says the name I received when I was outdoored
With my cut umbilicus used in tapping at the door is not enough!
One of his daughters who is already grown up
Is called Marta; the son is Gulyelmo.
Is Marta a grandmother's name?
What on earth is the meaning of Gulyelmo?
He claims that Acholi names are primitive names.
My praise-name is Eliya Alyeker
I ate the name of a hero, Chief of Payira
Eliya, son of Awich Aliker.

> He's gone to Lumule, but will return
> His mother is anxiously awaiting his return, saying
> Please bring back Alyeka for me to behold.
> Alyeka is already in Palabek
> His mother watches the path, expecting him.

Heroic names are given to leaders of girls
For they are heroines, they are princesses:
These are respected girls, superlative performers,
Excellent dancers, leading soloists:
They are the ones who are given bull names.
My mother had *Kabaka* bestowed on her:
She received the name of the king of Baganda:

Heroic names are not selected from one's clan.
The bull name my aunt ate was 'Tanner':
The British Captain the Lamogi killed
In their rebellion in the Guruguru caves.
Mucha Ali, the famous son of Patiko
The first priest in Acholi-land, lies well respected;
This son of Ywaa, who surpasses him?
Many girls aspire to be named Mucha!
Anying Yona, and La-loyo
All these names are given to leading girls
Names of those who've shown leadership qualities
These are the ones heroic girls receive
Girls who are active and hot like pepper
Who are itchy and wild like honey bees.
Is Chichilia a bull's name?
Is it the name of a leader of girls who is active?
Benedeta, is that a family name?
Is it a family name inherited from the past?

Apiyo and Achen are sacred names;
We respect twins more than last kids.
You do not mistreat twin-borns
Their birth rites, and even their burial rites, are different;
Twins are buried in twin-mouthed pots.
Okelo is he who comes after spirit kids.
In our custom mothers of twins do not eat the slippery eels.
Ajok is not given one's daughter because she is a witch;
But she's named because her fingers are more;
Like the boy Ojara; or perhaps her fingers are fewer.
But, even Ojara is still respected.
Odoch is a boy born the wrong way out,
Who came out of the womb feet-first.
She who is called Adong
Is so named because her dead father left her in the womb.
Okot is not given to those born during rains
Nor necessarily because he was born during the rainy season:

But because his umbilicus held the translucent rain.
She who is evil-hearted her daughter is called Akwir,
She who is famed for killing people using deadly venoms,
Her daughter would be called Anek - the killer
Because she's a witch, a poisoner of people.

Should a man give the name Bitek to his son
That's because he reckons though he's still weak, he'll become
    strong;
Because, as they say, slowly the determined man gathers
    strength.
Others give the name Oling to their sons
Meaning thereby that though his son is still suckling
Let the world laugh, he'll wait quietly for surprises.
Some African names are names of woes:
Alobo is a rebuke to the world that has mistreated the parents
Obur is 'the grave', Ayiko is 'I have buried', Lawoko is
    'the world'
Ru-piny is 'daily suffering', Too is very 'death'. Woko-rach
That is a dirge; fate has given her a basket to fill with corpses;
It means: misfortune has knelt on her, pressing her down!
It means: misfortune started haunting her when she was young;
The large basket is for harvesting her dead relatives.

    I'm perching on a tree branch like a bird
    I am like a monkey squatting on a tree
    Woe is me, fate is pressing hard on me
    What can I say?

My father's name was Otoo Leng'a-moi
He earned his heroic name killing the Galla
For the 'moi' name is earned with the spear
And the gun, the sword, or sharp knife.
My grandfather's manner of killing earned him the name
    Lutany-moi
He was war leader, a hero, son of Anyala.

Now Jekchon, is that a spirit-child's name?
Iriko Gulyelmo, is that a mourning name?
Bichenychiyo, is that a praise name of foreigners
Which girls use for praising him while dancing?

We welcome the first son with the name Okang
For he's the first child to come out of the womb
Besides, he has demonstrated that his mother is not a barren girl.
He will officiate in the shrine, he's well respected
His word is law: he decides who gets what.

The boy who comes after the first is called Oboi:
They fight, they play, they come together, that's sibling rivalry.
After Oboi comes Odai.
And the last child is referred to as Chogo.
Should you hit his head, his mother would get cross
For he's her beloved child.

Now, these new baptism names, who knows their meanings?
The names that people get after reading in the Church
The European names that are given to innocent kids
On baptismal day in the big churches
They sound cacophonous to my ears.
They sound like rusty tins
Into which rainy drops drip on and on.
If you call me by them, I won't answer!

My husband (and all the Christian priests) cannot enlighten me on the Biblical creation story

When we were attending Evening Classes
We recited the Messengers' Signs
We sang Our Father who is above the Sky
We learnt Good Morning Mary

> You are lucky among women
> You are full of grasya

We learnt that Cleanness should remain with the Father

> Should rest on the Son, and on the Clean Ghost
> As it started from the word go
> Up to now, daily henceforth, for ever and ever, Amen.

We sang the Yes Prayer, and the Love Prayer
Trust Prayer, and the Gift of Angels
The Decalogue and God's Messages Ten.

Free enquiry is anathema to Christian priests!
Be they Protestant or Catholic priests:
You brook a quarrel by asking questions on faith.
The White priests hate you as much as the African ones:
They are all united against Christian doubts.

Upon mounting the pulpit
They shout their sermons non-stop.

If you missed a word, or couldn't get the sense
They rush away after the sermon:
They have no time to spare for your quest.
Straightaway they begin to take collections

Saying:

> Those who sow little
> Will reap little rewards;
> Those who sow much
> Will reap a rich harvest.

Feel free to give as much as you can:
God's pleasure goes to generous people.

Does earthly wealth book for one
Heavenly vacancy, I wonder?
Those who grabbed, extortioned, and are corrupt
Is their candidature for heaven guaranteed?
Where do we stand, we ordinary people?
Will God the Father be a hostage to fat-bellied tycoons?
Sitting on His left and right, front and back?

The gray-haired V.I.P.s that we know
With double chins and fat purses
They who are also honoured by God's men
Will they be the ones to enjoy heavenly peace?
Heat does not suit their nature:
Used as they are to comfortable life,
To palatial feasting in our version of heaven.
Want, and life of pain, is alien to them:
Any other life will be Hell to them!

If you are stingy with your gift, so will you be rewarded:
It is up to you to choose how much you give.
But should you cultivate a small field
Don't be surprised if your harvest is nil.

*　　　　*　　　　*

Catechists abhor enquiring minds.
Don't think the Catholic padre is any different:
He will fight you for entertaining doubts.
The Mother Superior is even worse:
Fierce she is, very ferocious indeed:
Like a wounded buffalo, she is.
Protesters deserve to go to Hell, she says.
She'll call you all types of names
Shouting at the top of her voice.

Black Catholics are especially cross
Blaming Martin Luther for the rift
That produced Protestants: argumentative people
Who doubt what the church fathers had ordained.
Fathers wear themselves out, defending the faith.

    *   *   *

We sang the Symbols of the Carriers of Word
Shouting like parrots, without understanding a thing!
At night I sought its meaning in vain
I have not got a clue. But who will enlighten me?

Father and Mother Superior are no help:
Full of bile, adverse to clearing doubts.
Why are they so cross? Did I forbid them getting married?
If you pester them, they hit you on the head!

Good kids take for granted what is taught
They lap it up like dog and vomit:
Like death who kills Miss World and leper;
Like the rubbish dump, they accept anything;
Like a latrine, they accept dung and diarrhoea.

Kids who say "Yes" to all
Without a fleck of doubt

Are favoured by priests and given sweets;
Are given rides in cars, are never left to walk.

*   *   *

We recited Symbols of the Carriers of Word
Like wild turkeys, we clucked on and on ....
The teacher led the way in shouting hard
We followed suit outdoing him.

    I accept God the Father, who has powers over all
    The maker of Sky and Earth ...

My mother was a potter of renown
Large, small, and tall pots;
Water pots and smoking pipes: she made them all;
Round pots of beauty and cooking pots open.
She dug the clay from Oyitino stream
Where there is a particular spot known for its clay
As I learnt, when I was young.
Later, I even accompanied mum to the place.

God dug the clay for creation from where?
The silt for moulding the Sky, where is it obtained?
The soil for making Earth, where is it dug?
The pit for the creation clay, by which river is it?

Now, after getting the clay from the river
Mother would leave it to mature for a day or two.
Later on, she would knead it ready for making pots
Producing durable wares which fire well:
Small pots with smooth long necks;
Food vessels strong and red;
Comely cooking pots, pleasing to see.

Now, when the Sky was not yet there
And Earth was not even there

Neither were Stars
Nor the Moon ...
When not even a single thing existed
Where did God stay?

Where did God dig the clay from?
The clay for the Sky, the soil for the Earth, and the Moon;
The clay for making the twinkling stars, was dug from where?
Which river has that type of clay?

Now, when He was digging the earth-making clay
Where did God the Chief stay?
When He had brought out the clay
Where did He deposit it to mature?
When He was busy kneading it for use
On what table-land did He place it?

Ochol my husband is a university graduate,
He has studied much and is widely read.
But when you ask him a question, he says you are disturbing him.
He becomes angry, and starts deriding you
That you are wasting his time
With your peasant's silly requests:
The questions betraying empty heads.
My man says I have little understanding:
I don't look intelligent enough
To get any meaning from his explanations.
For, an interpreter would be needed for what he said:
He speaks in parables, wisdom words.
Why should he waste his time
Talking to the uninitiated
Clod of earth? It is unbecoming
For him to talk to me.

My man would turn his back to you, abandoning you
Barking like a beast hurt: protecting his flanks.

The Catholic Father would twist his beard, threateningly
The Catholic Sister would cross herself, confessing faith!

I have tried and failed to get sense out of it all!
I have cried in defeat, my head has ached.
But who will help me? Where turn for help?

I am not bashful by nature;
I am not afraid, nor am I shy:
To ask a question is not to sin.
I am not easily fooled
Neither can I be shut up
By threats of consignment to hell.

My unrequited search for knowledge chokes me
My head aches, my heart pains
The veins in my head throb .....
I have turned the matter over and over in vain
My eyes have turned red with tears
I have failed to fathom its meaning, I am mad
And shake with rage!

* * *

When god was not even there
Before He had moulded Himself
What was there?

Before the Sky and Earth were made
Neither were Stars
Nor the Moon
Before God was even made
When He had not yet fashioned Himself
Where did He get the clay for His work?
The soil for self-creation, where did He get it?
From the mouth of which river did he scoop it?
Now, when God was not yet there

Before He had even made His own head
Or His eyes
Or His hands
Or His feet
Before He even had a heart:

How did He find the creation clay
Since He had not created His eyes yet?
Which river yielded the God-making clay?
How did God dig the creation clay?
How did He hold the digging stick
Without the aid of created hands?

How did He wield the mallet for pounding clay
Without the aid of created hands?
When He was not yet even there?
When He was busy scooping out the clay for self-creation
With whose feet did He stand firmly by the stream?

Where did the Lord God get His head
To conceive the idea of self-creation?
For His initial mental explosion
Whose head did God borrow?

Where did God acquire the hands for creation?
His hands for self-creation, where did He get them?
How did He make His hands for making Himself?
When He did not even have hands yet!

I thought hard and much
But I could not understand them:
I thought about them on the way to the river, or collecting
    firewood,
I thought about them when spreading grains to dry
I thought about them grinding millet into flour
Or errly in the morning when going to dig through the dewy path,

Even at night, they kept me wide awake!
My thinking came to a stop, I became cold and numb
I changed from side to side, restless and groaning.

The questions are many and keep on coming
Once you start asking them, they flow like water
Everlasting they are, like Hell-fire; many like grass.

*   *   *

You'd wish you had nothing else to do but think
These thoughts over and over in your head.
You'd wish you got a man of deep understanding
And not merely bookworms like Ochol my man
Who acquired enough information to impress
Market women and those unschooled
Shouting their little knowledge for all to hear.

You'd wish you had a true companion
Who'd understand your questions;
Who'd teach you step by step;
Who'd tolerate your slow progress in learning:
Who'd not lose patience
Who'd work hard to clear your horizon
And not make you lose confidence in yourself.

This matter of the birth of Christ, for example:
They say Mary had had no affair with Joseph
Whereas he had already paid the bride price.
When an Acholi girl has accepted a man
She gives him a keepsake, and trysts
To test him at night.
They romance and play about:
Perchance, she conceives that very night:
A bit early, but no shame.
But when they say that Jesus was conceived without sex

I don't understand it at all!
No wonder Catechists don't like me a bit.
They don't like the questions I throw at them.
They'd leave one to go astray, rather than return her to the fold.
Is it because they're equally ignorant, or simply obstinate?
I can't tell: except that they hate doubts.
Religious leaders hate to be questioned on faith.

My husband rejects me claiming I do not know hygiene and the new explanations of disease and death

Ochol hates me, he claims I know no hygiene
He avers that I do not know how to tend the sick
And that I do not know curative effects of quinine
Besides, that I was not taught how to maintain good health
And that I do not know the uses of iodine.

He quarrels, he says, because my mother frequents divination
He even claims my grandfather was a famous diviner:
We are therefore poles apart, besides, he fears what people
     would say
For, it is said, my mother has very powerful juju.
Besides, the poisons our women use are very hot
He claims my grannie had introduced a new killer acid
And a variety of Ma'di poisons for decimating kids!

He says I encourage guests to come and stay
Especially the villagers who shouldn't reach his home
Who are dirty and are followed by rowdy, noisy flies;
He claims my old relatives give off such a stench
For they are all sickly and scratch themselves all over:
Some are lepers and others cough from T.B.
Which diseases he fears would infect our kids.

He utters all that comes to his mind without respect
For relatives who are around. When a heavy storm is coming
Ochol urges the villager guests to pack and go.

73

My husband says my aunt's head is grown wild
She should not visit me. He turns away even mothers-in-law
Including those with healthy young kids.

His own mother too, he chases away, saying she spits a lot
Making the place dirty. Besides her inner garment's infested
        with worms and fungus!
He is sure her head is full of dirt and lice!
As soon as visitors have come, Ochol is up in arms!

Whenever Ochol begins to complain about foods
You begin to wonder whether he earns money or sand:
He complains that his uncle is eating too much;
He fears no avuncular curse nor behaves like a grown-up
It all makes him light, reduces his public esteem.

He forbids our kids to visit my mum
Because he says grandmothers spoil the kids
By feeding them all the time without respite;
Besides, he cares not for the aunties' teachings
Which he says would lead the kids into foolish ways
Into paths of sickness, poverty and ignorance
The wise teachings of the African he does not want to know.

My man despises me for fearing the *Abiba* ghost
He says there's no flying kite with fire at its arse:
He says it is all hallucination and superstition of the masses
Which makes them think they have seen wonders.
He threatens to beat me for consulting the seers renowned.

He would not like to hear of the diviner priest;
He once gave me a beating for removing lower incisor teeth
He explains away the poisoned-hair, as mere intestinal tic
He accuses diviners for being liars, embezzlers of funds
Who mesmerise the foolish and ignorant with their tricks.
He says all their drugs are dug from the ground

And are served in dirty and very old water gourds
Or unwashed calabash used for native bread
In small gourds that look rough and unseemly like
    bewitchers' tools
Above all, he says the calabash is filled to the brim!
There is no measure for enough or excess dosages all the time.

When the small-pox epidemic has invaded the home
Ochol does not go to the ancestral shrine to seek divine
    intervention
And has made all his daughters wear the rosary;
He vituperates against the wearing of the elephant-hair necklace
And has barred me from wearing the edible rat's claws
Or the rhino horn, or the monitor lizard's bones!

He forbids us planting the auspicious lily
Has banned the exorcism of the demons that haunt my life
Especially when their season for exorcism is on.
Even when I am struck by a serious disease
And am confined to bed, sometimes with the evil eye;
Or when the ailment comes from breaking a taboo,
My husband forbids the killing of the sacrificial goat.

He puts it down to the superstitious ways
Ignorant ways of backward people
People left in darkness, those with little ken
He says he has no faith in superstitious beliefs.

Diseases should all be taken to a doctor, he says
Including poisoned feet or leprosy sprinkled on one:
My husband does not want the diviner to find the killer or cure;
Including the onset of madness as prelude to *Omara* priesthood
Or the signs of God *Odude's* priest-possession, or the
    evil *Ayweya*
Even the attack by *Rubanga,* the God that twists the spinal cord

Or the jealous river Gods that interfere with conception
Stopping girls from bearing kids when the full dowry is paid!

My husband forbids the music of the exorcism rattle;
Or the beating of the sacred drum for appeasing twins;
And the ritual hedge *Okango* he pulls it out before sinking roots.

He claims that demon-exorcism came from Palwo
And that it is a lecherous dance that makes women loose;
That it spreads gonorrhoea, especially as it is a night dance
And women stay there, keeping late hours;
Its songs are immoral he says, they teach women disrespect.
Above all, believers in it turn their backs on hospitals.
At times when Ochol is stirred to action
He behaves as if he's back from a drinking bout
He grabs a torch and threatens to burn down the family shrine
Making you wonder if he is bewitched.

*   *   *

It is true I do not know the English names of diseases
The whiteman's hygiene was not taught to me
So that looking after the sick
In the European way is foreign to me.
Our traditional diagnosis of a sick child is this:
It will be febrile and have a runny nose,
It will lose pluck and be generally debilitated:
To know that this child is sick, I don't need to read a book:
The skin would have become rough and ashen.

When the sick child cries, it will have enforced breath
It would turn pale as if powdered with ashes
The heartbeat would be jerky
And it would lose all appetite for food
Its tongue would be dry, it would anger quickly;
It would be weak, with a pitiably exhausted look
Its bodily hair would stand on end, the lips dry and cracked,

76

Paleness and languor would characterise the sick
With tears running down its nose, obvious signs of weakness.
The whole body would feel hot to the touch
But still the child would go near a fire, when the sun is hot!

Finding out how hot a child is by the glass machine defeats me
For, my hand trembles when I handle it
And if I succeeded in doing it, I wouldn't know how to read it.
Well, after it is measured does it stave off death?
When one's turn for the final journey has come, there's
        no stopping
However much one struggles against it:
Whichever doctor you bring will do nothing
Death will drag you to the grave: a narrow room.

With me, when a child is sick
I struggle, I try all the African drugs
And when the sickness is abating
I take a cock to the effective medicineman.

When a baby has constant bouts
And the body is hot with fever and malaria
Which have broken him down
In his infancy, arresting growth
I know straightaway that there's a reason behind it:
My co-wife has hurt him through her magic.

Should a child have diarrhoea, plus cough
Has lost weight till its clothes are too large
That is because his stool has been used to hurt him
Or his hair is given to the river Gods to harm him:
These are acts of enemies, or jealous kin.

Should a child remain weak and cannot crawl
That's because its vital powers have been captured.
That calls for immediately consulting the diviner

77

To find out who it is that has done this heinous deed
Who it is who is murder-bent.

What's wrong with divining the causes of death?
What sin is there in telling the future by sandals' use?
Why should I be the butt of people's abuses
Simply because my father takes precaution by examining
The bird's message before going to hunt the next day?
Or he attends and interprets the message of the woodpecker
    and others?
You don't go to wage a war without interpreting the auguries
Our elders read the intestines of goats first.

When a group of girls are walking to the well
Or when they are coming back from gathering wood
Or they are going to play with fellow youths
And the snake bites your daughter at the end of the line
What sort of misfortune is this?
Other people's children go unmolested
The snake waits specially for yours. Why is that?

In the heat of war, your son is speared to death
The spear goes through the breastplate to the heart:
Others' kids go unscathed through showers of barbs
That come raining down from the enemy bows
Broken twigs do not even scratch them!

Your child is sought by lightning and hit in the house!
In the hunting ground, others' kids skirt the danger zone
But yours heads straight like a thing possessed
Pushes through the grass, spear in hand
Till he reaches the buffalo and is gored to death!

All these manners of death reveal something.
When your uncle mildly curses you, you wet your bed

And your heart palpitates unimpeded
Give him the appeasing cock and you are OK

Should your mother lift up her breasts
And ask you: "Didn't you suckle these?"
Should your father lift up his penis
Realise straightaway that these are deadly matters!

To wrestle with your father is a forbidden thing
Mothers are not for despising, nor for abusing
Because it was that woman and her husband
Whose union brought you into this world.

Look back at all the stool and brine
And the sicknesses and vomits you poured out
On your mum; at fire burns she had
As she cooked for you, and all the feeding
And the jealousy, witchery and divinations;
When co-wives refer to you as the lucky one
Even when you are an only child, they say your mother has
a brood.
Hence however worn-out and flabby your mother's breasts look
They are the ones you suckled and sustained you till you could
eat;
Even if your father has lost his sight and is totally blind,
Even if he is deaf or has lost his wits;
Even if his legs are reedy and skeletal
When he rebukes you, you say 'thank you' and do not retort!
Because, he stands before you like the solid mahogany tree
To which you are a mere creeping plant, climbing up to reach
the sun!

Mothers should never be provoked to anger
Lest they expose their private parts!
If, in your ignorance you push your mother
To swear against you using ashes

You'll find all you have ever sought!
You'll lose your senses, your body will become pale;
And feeble-minded. Until the curative herb is applied
A goat is sacrificed, and your mother and uncle
Have reconciled with you, become one, once more loving
You will not become sane again!

If that act of atonement is not done, you'll
Walk in a daze, like a castrated billy goat!
Such afflictions are unknown to hospital doctors!
The curses of mothers and uncles
The anger of fathers, or desire to be loved
The key for all these are found in the ancestral shrine.

If a woman should break a taboo
Or a child hit another who is passing out dung,
If a bad woman has brought home the vengeance ghosts
But death has found no cause for revenge
And has reverted to destroying the bringer instead
And is killing kith and kin one by one
And the number of the dead swells beyond all counts;
If in the communal hunt your men's spears
Miss their target, and the hunters return home empty-handed;
When the sun shines non-stop and drought settles on earth
So that not even a handful of harvest is got
Not even enough beans for titbit ......

Whenever such calamities strike a home
Elders repair to the shrine and offer foods and drinks
And invoke dead living ancestors and spirits to ward off
    the attacks:

    Let the setting sun take all sufferings away!
    Let it take them away!
    Take, sun-set, take with you all evil as usual!
    Let it take all evil away, as usual!

The fatted meat and millet bread is offered to the ancestors
Everybody prays for peace and reconciliation
Marks are made on the chests of participants
Chyme is sprinkled on all around bringing blessings to all.

Entreaties to the ancestors are made: women should conceive
Bumper harvests should follow, hunters should kill, food
    be in plenty.
The eldest woman, now tottering on three legs
Blesses all: let the hunters' spears hit their targets
For spears of high repute deserve to do their works
Even if it is hitting a fox's hole, let it be on target:
Spears should not rust from inaction:

    The spear that is hard
    Spears the granite rock
    The spear that I love
    Cracks the rock
    The lone hunter has not returned
    I'll await him on the rock-top
    The master hunter's spear is strong
    I await his return.

If the evil person has poisoned your hand
Or if death is buried under your threshold
Because of envy, jealousy and hatred
When the voodoo person wants to cast a spell on you
He'll dance round your house, the witches' dance:

He'll be all covered in ashes, with copper-bangle on arm
He'll bury dead frogs in your roof
And bury dead chameleons in the hard sesame garden.
Now, will you just sit and await the certain death?
Do you wait till death has struck and people begin to mourn?
Don't you resist by asking diviners for counter-measures?
Don't you trap the night-runner by drawing an ashen line

So that when he jumps across it, he'll fall and be caught?
And in the morning he'll be found bloated up and impaled
With a long wood or iron right to his throat?

Do you just sit and wait?
Tell me truly: don't you struggle and contest the issue?
Do you wait till the hoe digs the grave?
Do you wait till misfortune settles in,
Has conquered you, and taken away the ones you love?
Do you ignore it until your kith has died?

*   *   *

When all the girls around turn their backs to you;
Whenever you touch the hand of this one she disengages
    and goes away
You see that beautiful one there and plan to propose to her
But when you meet her in the youth dance
And introduce matters of love, she breaks off and runs
Won't you go and search for her the love potion?
Won't you try attracting her by the lily roots?
Won't you search for the newly born pup's horn and
    uncle's blessing?

My husband hates me claiming that I do not know hygiene
That I am still stuck in the superstitions of old
In addition, I do not understand the import of the new religion
Therefore he won't have anything to do with traditional belief.

He says I do not know the rules of health
Claiming I mix up causes of sickness with superstitious beliefs
Besides, I don't even know the names of germs that
    bring diseases!

Ochol makes my head ache with his cheap acquisitions
Besides, he mixes indecorous abuses and insults;
He claims he has studied all things in depth,

That he studied side by side with whites all manners of things.
He's unlike us who walk in the dark, or a hole deep and dark
Who do not know what is good and what is bad.

But, my husband's teachings are useless!
These are words of pride, words of deceit
Stories for brow-beating village girls; joking games.
His knowledge is thin, good only for winning cheap arguments.
All that Ochol says has no foundation!

My husband has allowed party politics to bring enmity between him and his younger brother

With the party politics that's now before us
My husband crosses ridges like the he-goat in rut:
He's up early as if going to cultivate your field
He's astir and on the move before John the Baptist awakes.
He knocks from house to house like a beggar;
On entering a house, he checks what's on the table!
As if I don't feed him well. When he's gone campaigning
He'll not be back till the sun is completely gone.

He'll be back for a moment only before
He's gone again, to a party meeting, he says, for
A select committee at the headman's house.
They'll be there the whole night. I wish
My mother knew what man I married!

My husband has made party politics his main job:
He's alert and vigilant like the fowler with his nets;
Party work is now the hive from which honey is got
It is now his cotton field and sesame garden
When he finally arrives he lies that the lorry had broken down
Most times he sleeps away, leaving me all alone!

He says they are fighting for independence!
That they're fighting for self-rule and peace!
When they're together you hear: *Uhuru! Uhuru!*
Complaining that the whiteman has us all imprisoned!
This *uhuru* they shout about, what's its meaning to you?

They say they're after casting ballot and direct election
That they'd like to unite the Acholi and the Lang'i
The Ma'di and the Lugwari to all live in peace!
They say the Alur and the Teso and Baganda, all
Together with the Banyankole and Banyoro tribes
Should all unite together with the Banyaruanda tribe,
And that the Padola should understand the Batoro.

They say the whiteman should return to his home
That the whiteman was bad, he had introduced imprisonment
And forced labour which is bad and slave-like;
They no longer want the communal granary.

They claim the coloniser doesn't tell us all;
And that the whiteman is a robber, expert thief of wealth,
That they beat us by telling sweet lies like a wooer
While in truth they despise us, and believe we're all
    uncivilised.

*   *   *

I listen to this party talk and it does not satisfy me.
To begin with the party uniforms are variegated in colour and cut:
Some are dressed in long robes like witch-doctors of God
But they're rough and wild with one another.

Ochol dons a green robe laced with white
He stalks stealthily, he moves heavily
Like a rogue chimpanzee. He blows his whistle
And beats the gong, calling for a quick assembly of men.

His brother is robed in black and red
He resembles a chief justice about to commit a man to death;
Or like the red finch. He shouts like a railway engine
And struts majestically, like the rogue elephant.

Ochol is the head of the Dee-Pee party
Whose patent greeting is the clenched fist;
His brother heads the You-Pee-See party
And their registered sign is the open palm.

Dee-Pee - what does it really mean?
Their top brass belong to the Catholic Church though!
Congress - what type of religion is that?
Is Uganda People's Congress a Protestant party?

Congress - what does it really mean?
Ochol and his brother do not share food together!
Even water, they partake of it in common in the river!
Ochol never enters his brother's house, as if

There's a family feud that is not settled yet.
It's as if there is a murder case still awaiting appeasement
It is as if they fear to incriminate themselves.
Ochol and his brother are now diametrically opposed
Party politics has broken family bonds, has brought us new evils.

Ochol forbade me strictly ever to joke with my brother-in-law
Not because he fears we would romance and go to bed
Not because I have an open welcome for all flirting men
But because a joking relationship might revive family bonds.

Are these advance tastes of unity under *uhuru*?
The well-being that self-rule is bringing, are these their
    fore-tastes?

When he launches out criticising his brother, you'd bow
    in shame!
It is as if they never suckled from the same breasts;
It is as if they never came from the same womb,
When in fact it was Ochol who vacated the womb for his brother

86

And when they were both young, tending family goats
They were inseparable like twins, like eye and nose!
They were so much in love they shared tit-bits and secrets!

Ochol claims that his brother's a liar
Who asserts and defends lies and has wild mad eyes!
That his brother is a mere shell, a huge imbecile
From whom all trust should be removed.
He alleges that his brother is plotting his demise!
He apostrophises his brother as: "That man"; "my sworn enemy"
And urges us all not to heed his words
For 'that man' has collected lots of money and guns
And has hired hooligans to be his henchmen!
Ochol talks like a man in trance, with eyes wild and blazing!

He alleges that his brother wants to bring home communism.
What type of animal is this thing called communism?
He charges that Congress would disemploy all the Catholics;
Besides, they'd appropriate all land, schools, and wives
Including goats and chicken, and even bicycles
These would all become Congress property. They are enemies
Confusers, thieves, and liars who waste one's time.

When Ochol's brother has his turn at abuse
He's loud and piercing like the lead small drum
He asserts that Dee-Pee is the party of Catholic priests
It is the party of incompetents and ignorants like hens.

He says Catholics are all blockheaded
All they do is dictated to them by Italians;
That the Dee-Pee is a party for fools!
That they'd give all land to poor whites
Who have no place in their own lands
And who have come to our land in the guise of catechists
When in fact they've no qualifications. He claims Ochol
    has been captured by them.

Through all sorts of prayer, and kneeling down before the
    whiteman.

When you hear it, you doubt your intelligence!
You hold your mouth in disbelief and cry!
So, this is what money can do?
Even against your own brother you rage
And charge like the hyena newly delivered!

Party politics resembles cutting up the buffalo:
If your chest is weak you're edged aside.
If your knife is blunt you'll end up with offal
And return home everybody's laughing stock.
If you are a coward they'll keep you afar with threats.
You return home empty-handed and jeered by women.
Your grabbing mates will amass the fated meat
They'll return home blowing their horns and flutes
But you'll walk silently, crest-fallen like a defeated cock
And sit quietly like the sinful wife, or sit tail-tucked like a dog.
Daily, you'll subsist on greens when others are eating meat
Your kids will get thin, and chase flying insects for food
Their only source of protein-meat; others' kids would be
    bonny and smooth.
Others' wives would be fat, with shaky buttocks as they moved
For they're fed on fatted meats and juicy humps,
They'd be healthy , well-developed and their wounds would
    heal quicker.
The stomach is the sole reason for people joining parties
Party politics is the fast road for getting a job
Especially when one owned nothing before
Especially to those who had never tasted honey before
And others who had grown up as orphans.

Party politics is not suited to those who are bashful:
One concocts big lies without fear or shame
One makes improbable allegations without qualms

All sorts of abuses one hurls them without respect
For mothers and fathers who might be around.
Party-rivals abuse one another even when mothers-in-law
    are around
They abuse one another openly before their sisters!
Because of the stomach, brother, poverty makes you say it all!

When the party bosses are around
My husband jumps about like a new bride
He moves from place to place, recommending himself
He hurries up and down, spreading rumours everywhere
He behaves like the woman burying her co-wife
To every trite remark, he cries out: "Chief, that's great!"
And proceeds to laugh as though fun-loving, whereas he's
    a miserly man;
My people, the way party-posts are bought is truly demeaning!

My husband has a long list of those to be reported to the bosses,
Now, look at his confusion brought about by party-bosses!
Everybody else is bad, except he, he alone
Who else surpasses him in working hard, in being good
In readiness to work, in following orders, and winning members?
In alertness, defending the cause, and gathering news?
To top it all: he loves party bosses so!

He claims that the broad masses call him boss
Besides, when he talks, they all listen to him!
Ochol claims he's not proud, but a humble man.
He points to other party members who have already deserted
And gone and started their own party for fools,
But, his rivals have few followers; most of the people
    remained with him
He's the acknowledged leader whose fame extends everywhere!

    *   *   *

When my husband Ochol has mounted the platform
Bell and drum music will din the market place
There would be many people, some on hill tops
They'd be closely packed, like celebrants at the palace of a chief.

My man would open his book and read his speech
He'd read a few lines and wave his flywhisk!
Punctuated by women's yodelling and men's ululation
Saliva would scatter in every direction!
From time to time you'd hear *'Uhuru!' 'Uhuru!'*
Uhuru has become the new-found God now.
When my husband is fully launched
He resembles the wood-pecker, or the bird's mother-in-law.
The barbs he lets fly make your body itch
His words are hot like ripe boils on the arse.
He'll talk on, non-stop, going on from topic to topic
Resembling the spinster talking to herself and angry with
        the world!
Some of his points throb like a deep ulcer full of pus.

My husband shouts till his voice is cracked
claiming they want unity to better increase our lot.
That they're pursuing *uhuru* without altercations
That they want to bring peace and love
They're fighting against evil thoughts and poverty
That they're against enmity and separation
They'd like all Acholi to live in peace
That they should live like brothers, in total friendship!

When he has waved his fly-whisk you hear: Peace! Peace!
What he says is sweet like wild honey, like a sweet fruit.
If you had not known the division in the homestead
If you did not know that his home is no more
If you did not know of the chaff and rubbish
And the poverty and desecration that party politics has brought
If you're ignorant of the hatred and spiritual unrest

90

And the resultant suffering that people have borne
Whilst party-heads feed on honey daily
Whilst the masses feed on smell and gnawing discarded bones
You would conclude that Ochol is indeed the leader.
Whilst the common man feeds on smell and discarded bones
The bosses stuff their pockets full of notes,
The abused voters cover their corny feet in leather sandals!

*　　　*　　　*

Party propaganda indeed resembles wooing!
It is merely for looking for a place of wealth
Most of it is pure fabrication
It is all calculated to pave the way, to meet a need!

But, after they have been rewarded they make themselves scarce.
When they have been voted to high posts
You'll never see them again; they will be here and there!
But when election time is come round again
Then they would return like the kites from the north:

The kites have come back
Dry season is around!

Party politics is simply for deciding who's to rule
Like the contest between the red and grey finch
You launch an all-out attack against friend and foes.
Countrymen, this party era that is now upon us
Has brought with it all manner of evils.

The Dee-Pee party, how does it differ from the You-Pee-See?
Ochol claims that they're fighting for independence
His brother too wants independence, peace, and education!
Ochol claims he wants health and hates enemies of health;
His brother says he wants to see an increase of wealth.
Ochol says he wants more schools to be built;
His brother insists on more maternity wards and leprosaria.

Why don't they then combine forces against enemies of man?
Why don't they put their resources together
In order to defeat ignorance and disease?

You-Pee-See differs from Dee-Pee in what ways?
What are the fundamental differences between Dee-Pee and
Congress?
What are all the party-leaders really after?
Brother, does this contest make sense to you?

*   *   *

As for me the party propaganda does not tally well
Most of it is couched in foreign tongues:
Pipul Kongres, komunis, uhuru and the rest!
Like the train, they steam ahead without anybody
        understanding them!

Maybe party politics will bring us some peace
Only when the party leaders have turned to love:
They should not throw their rivals into jail
To show how powerful they are.
They should control their senseless hot tempers
Jealousy, and fears like thieving dogs!
If they're fighting to improve everybody's lot
If they're fighting against hunger and disease
If they're fighting against ignorance and lack of wealth
What stops them combining forces?
Why should Ochol treat his brother like a beast?

Now, all my sisters-in-law are wearing weeds
They're mourning the death of their home, which party
        politics has brought.
They are mourning the jealousy and hatred that party
        politics has brought.

Now then, if ever an epidemic were to break out
If skin disease and yaws should pay us a visit
The remaining weak people will all be finished off
Because there is much division in the home already!
This is due to the legacy of party tug-of-war.

If the party bosses have dedicated themselves to developing
    our land
Why don't they discuss it in peace?
Family conferences, do people usually shout when holding them?
Don't elders deliberate at length, taking turns?
Whoever shouts in such discussions is possessed;
His sense has left him: he's beside himself!
For, that's not the way to make peace and communal
    understanding
The true leader is humble, at peace with all, listens to complaints!

My people, the enmity that has come between Ochol and his bro
Had it turned Ochol's mind against lack of wealth;
If the abundant enmity that exists between party leaders
Had been directed at increasing educational facilities;
If all manner of confusion and discord politics has brought
Had been directed against ill-health
By now we would have vanquished all the enemies of man!
Wealth would have spread like sand
And the fruits of *uhuru* would have reached every pot!

My husband has become a slave to European culture through reading their books

Hear my cries my people, I am mourning my man
Who is lost in the wilderness
Ochol has regressed, he flails about like a baby
The man does all things any, like a stranger.

My husband is now completely changed
Both in thoughts and acts my man is changed
He now heaps abuses on me
He even derides my mother, as if I was a killer.

When Ochol was still wooing me, those were the days!
His eyes were widely open and bright
He devoured my firm breasts with those eyes
He had not turned deceiver yet:
His ears were still open and alive
My man was still a homely companion
He was then respectful, and hated quarrels
Ochol my friend was a man yet.

The big bull was a Black man still
The chief's son was still a true Acholi indeed
The pride of his mother Agik of Okol
He was a black, Acholi, and true.

*   *   *

As for school education, Ochol has read a lot!
He has read wide, he has read deep;

94

He has read with the whites and is very clever indeed:
His books have filled our house up completely.

But these books have taken a heavy toll on my man
For in the oral traditions of his people Ochol is dumb
He then despises the ancestral heritage he does not know
Claiming all the ways of the blacks are evil!
He's blind to the beauty of his people
He hides his blindness behind goggles that are dark.

He is tone-deaf to Acholi songs:
Neither does he hear abuses and sarcasms foreigners heap
On African cultures as rubbish and uncivilised:
Ochol now behaves like the whiteman's watch-dog.

*   *   *

My husband's house is a thick forest of books.
Some are huge, and tall like the mahogany tree
Some are old, their barks are falling off and their smell is evil!
Some are soft, others are thin and tall;
Some have barks that have dried up and are harder than
        ebony wood;
Some are green in colour, others are red like blood:
They look gory like a man-killer's bespattered body.
The backs of some books are shiny and satin black,
Like the black mamba curled up on a tree.

There are illustrations on the backs of some books:
Frightening pictures of witches cover their backs
Baldness is galore, haggard faces and bearded men
All are pictures of dead intellectual men
Visages of ghosts, resembling the diviners we know.

*   *   *

The files and papers strewn on the scholar's desk
Intertwine like creeping plants in the bush,

Or like the parasitic banyan tree strangling its host!
Some lie flat on the table, others stand on ends
All tightly jammed together like a wooden fence.

My husband's house is a forest of books, it is dark.
Lightless, one gets lost; it is also damp!
A dank vapour issues from the ground, hot and acidic;
Mix this with dew-poison and foul water standing on leaves
These fumes will kill you if you stay too long in this place.
You will choke, the poison attacks you in the wind-pipe
Then numbs your nostrils , and parches your throat up.
You will never appreciate sweet smells again!
Your favourite vegetable dish now becomes insipid.
Do not tarry long in this evil place:
Its solid darkness will explode your eyes.
Birds' dung and gummy droppings from branches
Will seal your ear for ever:
You'll never appreciate again the moonlit serenades
Of marriageable girls singing songs of woe
And songs of love and songs of worry;
Songs critical of old men who are favoured
Collectors of wives, bald-headed men who have ready bride-price
One's parents' favoured suitors but most hated by nubile girls
Who cannot marry their sweet-hearts for lack of wealth.

You'll never more appreciate the Acholi song
For lulling children to sleep, which goes:

> Baby's mum cooks late at night:
> Blames you for being careless with her child
> When she had at last cooked her dinner.
> But when she's still busy
> You are praised for being a good nurse:
> Capable of whiling away the time with games.

This sweet nurse's song will mean nothing to you:
It will sound like bricks falling thick on roofs of zinc.

If you tarry long in this wizard's den
The various ghosts that reside in this our forest:
The ghostly conclave of all the white men and women
Who cry out if you favoured a certain book
The anguished spirits of the zealous writers of these books
Will adopt you for their own
And turn you into a zombie, just like Ochol.

*   *   *

My man has read deep and wide
But this very reading has also destroyed him
In the cultures of his own people he is quite in the dark
His left eye and his right eye are both dead.
He hides his blindness by donning goggles
That are as dark as he is blind.
How could he then see and appreciate the beauty of Acholi girls?

Bookworms have blocked his eardrums with thick gums.
When the dry surface of the gum crackles
Ochol jumps up and down dancing
Saying: 'How sweet is the lyre's song today!'

*   *   *

Ochol my man, you have read everything in depth
You have learnt all the knowledge of the world:
But, the wise read to learn, to repent and change:
They appreciate correction, and adjust to line.

Only a fool angers quickly: he's stunted!
He rushes into anything like a beast
Which is cornered and knows not the way out
When his faults are pointed out he does not change
And visits his mother-in-law indecently dressed.

97

Look here man, you're becoming a whiteman's dog:
To please the master is its first duty:
It guards the home at night, hunts game in the park;
Drives wild cats away, and lies down when told.

Whiteman's dogs are intelligent, they understand their masters
They are trained and obey strict orders
They are calm, and lie down when instructed
Especially at meal times
They wave their tails, then tuck them under.
They chase chicken from the table, awaiting their turn
Of mixed left-overs and huge bones
And pieces of bread soaked in soup.
They are fed well, they become strong.

Man raises a dog to guard his home,
To kill game to feed the owner's kids.
Dogs are there to please their owners.

My husband Ochol, you are the head of this home
You are chief in this house, you are master here.
It is unbecoming of you to appropriate foreign ways:
You are the prince of an ancient realm
You are not a slave, bought or born:
Your ancestral totem pole stands firmly in the shrine!
Why beg and fawn as if you were constrained?
When foreigners despise us do you simply sit and stare?

Indeed, Ochol, my man, you are now a slave renowned!
A beast of burden bearing both man and pack!
Why bear hard on me, friend Ochol
A prince, now turned slave?

You may not have known it, man, you are a slave
In thought, in manners, and even speech.

98

You are proud for nothing, your pants are wet:
A mere bladder into which urine collects.

How sad! A certain man I know
Has no garden of his own: he survives on fallen crumbs!
What permanence is there in borrowed things?
Do borrowed robes ever fit properly?
Bones choke dogs to death; apes die from aping!

Then why are you wearing a shirt?
Why don't you tie the skirt around your waist?
The string apron suits you best; just as the gomes dress.
Petties and frocks are now your dresses, my man turned woman.

*   *   *

Alas, this Home is dead indeed!
Finally close the gates then with the thorn trees
Our youth have all perished unmarried and unchilded!
Whereas this Home was famed far and wide!
Is there no one to save our land? To defend it?
Who, indeed? Who will come at the eleventh hour?
Who is man enough to do it? Is there anyone out there?

Does a single free-born still exist here now?
Or is the home left to slaves alone?
My people, will this storm ever clear?
Bile knots my stomach up, I am getting sick!

All our youth have perished one by one
Their manhood destroyed in the reading house
Their testicles crushed by the big books!
Where do we turn for help?

If my husband permits me to scour away the film of forgetfulness, the afflictions of apemanship; allows me to display the beauty of African culture before him and apologises to the ancestors for his senseless abuses, he may become whole again.

Listen Ochol, if you're still within reach
If your thread of life is not yet cut
If the blood still courses, however slowly
If the love for life is still with you, take heart,
    have some porridge.

Permit me to lift you up, here's fish soup
Persevere in regaining health, you'll get well.
Drink this *omwombye* root, however bitter
Take this sour hibiscus-leaf soup;
Chew some *lurono* root to loosen your tongue
When the *lukut* paste is mixed, scoop it.

Let sesame oil be dropped down your ears
So the thick gum that accumulated there is scooped out:
All the dust you collected from church and altar
Plus the rubbish gathered from books: rank pollutants!

Here's some water, it is tepid.
Let me pour it for you to wash the dirt from your face;
Throw the dark mystifying goggles away;
Now wash your face, the water won't burn you.

Scour away the daylight pus that closed your eyes:
The pus that formed whilst you closed your eyes in prayer;
Bring the rough *labikka* fruits so we can scrub his eyes with it
So the rotten blood can be lanced; bring the rhino horn
Let's drop its powder on the eyes to remove the cataracts
The thick accretion that blinded you from school can only be
    exorcised by a witch!
Your tonsils that have turned septic should be scrubbed clean
And all that shame you swallowed in the church should be
    retched out.
Pour down your throat raw fresh egg, or uncooked flour
If these would not induce eructation, then push your finger down
    your throat.

Rub clean your teeth with sand, scrape the dirt from your tongue;
Rinse your mouth with water, and eject the swallowed shame
    away,
Spit out all the abuse against us that the whiteman had taught you
And the spirit of insistent argument to back up a wrong cause.

And when you are cured, son of a bull,
Ochol my husband when you've regained your health,
Repair to the shrine of your fathers with an ox
Sacrifice it to the spirits, let the elders feed and drink;
Give the ancestors their portion of blood and beer
Let the elders spit their blessings on you
Let them intercede between the living and happy ancestors:
Entreat them to forgive you, beg them to arm you afresh
Let them overlook your past sins of insults and careless talk
So that no harm befalls you from here onward.
For, you sinned when you abused me as a mere village girl:
The same category encloses your grandparents, father and mum;
When you used to compare me to the rubbish in the refuse dump
You had thereby abused all your race including your sires.
You had simply relegated all African cultures to a dying past.

*   *   *

In my role as your elder wife
I have only one request to make:
It is not wealth I crave, though my position is dire;
It is not meat I seek, for I can still survive on greens;
If you want to deck my co-wife in the best of dresses
Lavish on her trinkets and all the jewels she needs;
Cover the walls of your zinc-house with the best cement:
I am comfortable in my grass-thatched hut.

What I beg of you, husband, is to unblock my way,
I beg you, Ochol, to give me the chance
I beg you, my man, not to run away from me
Give this girl the chance to display her skills.

Please don't stop me, my friend,
Please step aside so that I may come in
My *adungu* harp is tuned, with a song let me greet you
Let me pluck the strings for singing: "The mother of Awich
    expects her son"
Then let me sing for you: "The smallness of my lover is a
    small matter."

Don't stop me, please don't say *apana*
Let me praise you Chief, be kind.
Don't run away, nor go this way and that way.
Permit me first to pronounce my praise names!
I beg you my dear friend, dear brother give me chance
To display before you the wealth in your house.

You used to admire my elephant-necklace
My father had got it from Agoro in East Acholi.
When I graced my neck with a single strand
It made my neck long like the crane's;
When it pleased my heart, I wore many strands.
My father had desired it, he took pride in adorning me!

Inside my mother's house you used to move on your knees
All because of me: the whole front and back of me!
Because of me this bull used to shed bitter tears
He used to stay awake all night when I was in my prime.
He would never let a day go - this man - without seeing me.
You frequented our home daily, and never desisted when beaten!

Friend, don't think old age has reduced my beauty
Does the old guinea-fowl loose the baldness on its head?
Chum, tie on my legs the ankle-bells or *lachuchuku* rattles
Bring the *nanga* musician, and the calabash player should attend:
As they play let me display my expertise in Acholi dances
So know me more truly, so that you know
That the culture of your people is never forsaken.

Concluding Statement: The indigenous culture of your people you do not abandon

Pumpkins abandoned in homesteads are never uprooted
Remove weeds from beneath them if you're wise
Manure them with ashes and animal droppings
Keep the sharp edge of the hoe from them, give them chance.

If you really are the heir to your father's heritage
Pull out the weed, leave the pumpkins alone;
Uprooting the pumpkins is taboo: nobody does it.

If you are the true son of your father, Ochol
If you know what is good for you, dear brother,
Have a reverence for the pumpkin, respect it highly
You are old enough to know that the pumpkin is never uprooted!

Pumpkins in abandoned homesteads are never uprooted
For, they are food and not play-things.
Even if you are sated with a protruding anus
He who wastes food deserves to be shot.

You hypnotically admire others' achievements
Didn't they tend theirs with care and love?
You scramble for crumbs under foreigners' tables
But those are the fruits of their careful husbanding!
Your eyes pop out admiring other's attainments

104

Which they had cultivated carefully, year after year.
Ochol grabs with enthusiasm cultural artefacts of the whiteman
Which they had nurtured after years of trials and errors.

Pumpkin bole in an abandoned homestead is never uprooted;
For, from time immemorial, pumpkin has been the sustainer
    of life;
Even its leaves are boiled and eaten
The ripe fruit fills a big basket when sliced into shapes,
After they are dried, they are stored in granaries for later use.

Pumpkin seeds are tasty when roasted well
And salted; they're in vogue when the dry season is near.
Pumpkin fruit is easy to cook, and ideal for welcoming guests:
The more the guests, the more the pumpkin boiled.

Pumpkin bole in an abandoned homestead is never uprooted
For, nobody knows where he might seek shelter.
Who knows where he might be when the sun sets?
Where to knock, seek shelter for the night, who knows?

Pumpkin bole in an abandoned homestead is never uprooted
For, when the rainy season might commence is unknown:
Nor when guests might arrive, nor where they might seek shelter
Nobody has any prior knowledge of these, nor how to foresee them
The pumpkin is good for promoting life not for pulling down
And food is life, not for play,
Even when you're satiated, or it is already night!
Death from famine is worse than death from a gun!

Few people make it to the new homestead;
Death takes its toll all the time without any warning:
It hits you when you least expect it
It does not give you the chance for getting ready.

Even if you crouch behind the biggest buffalo shield;
Even if you crawl into the rat's secret hole;
Even if you have not come forth from mother's cosy womb;
Even if you hide in the great rocks' secret grotto;
Even if the mighty Agoro Hills are hiding you!

Even if you are a fast runner who never tires
You cannot flee from it, it follows you, fast like a demon
Death cannot be untied, cannot be shed like a shirt
The chase ends at death: life meets death when you're dead.

Death that ends life, its other name is 'Who does it refuse?'
When it summons, you leave food for the living
Who will inherit all that's left behind, like wealth or wives.
The pumpkin in an abandoned homestead is never uprooted
For the pumpkin is sweet, is tasty.
When night-time chances upon you in the ruins, you sleep:
You eat some pumpkin and feel homely away from home.

Therefore, however glutted you may be
Even if you are filled up to your throat
And walk like a pumped-up dummy with distended tummy,
Don't kick away the porridge calabash with your feet.
Don't break the pots when your stomach is bloated
And you are light-headed, swearing never to feed again!
If you have eaten, thank your gods, and go to sleep:
Don't look down on food, however sated you are,
Don't behave as if you are bewitched;
Do not play with fire near the granary
Where sesame, millet, or beans are stored:
For, one day's satisfaction is not enough.

For, that which is in your stomach is mere bubbles
Mere airsacks, welling up for belching.
After releasing the pressure once or twice
Your stomach will demand a fresh levy:

It will demand food with the ferocity of the man-eating lion
It brooks no delay, it metes out quicker reprisals
It is hotter than fire, hotter than pepper:
The hungry stomach is more ferocious than the lion.
Truly speaking, friend, what your stomach contains is gas
And should it be released the whole place would be fouled up!
All the same, man's fate is such that
Daily feeding ends only when we die.

*   *   *

That we must develop, I do accept:
Our land should also move ahead;
Water does not flow upstream
Human beings should not remain wild like animals.

But the big tree should sink its roots down
Deep into the ground, to withstand the buffeting winds.
A plant that squats without roots when the soil is soft
Should the thunderstorm come, it won't wait.

Pumpkin boles in abandoned homesteads are never uprooted.
Pumpkins in homesteads are never uprooted.
Pumpkins are not for uprooting! That's all!

Glossary

I have appended a glossary of words whose meanings are not obvious in the main body of the poem or whose scientific names would destroy the rhythm of the poem. Ideally, every poem does not need a glossary, especially translated poems. But since I had taken Okot to task for the omission of a glossary in 1967, I guess I need to produce one which explains the obvious or difficult words. Since the emphasis is on the fact that Lawino knows her fauna and flora (especially the flora with which she has daily commerce) we shall not insist on finding out if she knows them by Linnaean binominal nomenclature.

Abalo-pa-ng'a?	:	"Whose grain have I harvested prematurely?" Period preceding harvest when famine is most acute.
Abiba	:	Magical kite that is believed to fly at night with hot fire at its bottom, a witch's emissary and tool. (Alur origin?)
abwoga	:	a child prematurely born.
adung'u	:	a bow-like lyre wjth the string forming the letter Z, played over a down-turned calabash as resonator.
Ager	:	Period of dry-sowing of seeds.
arak	:	a strong spirituous distillate (waragi) which reached Acholi-land through the Arabs, from Arabic/Ki-Nubi.
awola yer	:	(poisoned-hair): some variety of whooping cough is attributed to a hair magically lodged inside the patient's lungs.

108

Ayweya	:	a variety of Jok - evil spirits - which harms people.
nying twat	:	praise names (bull-name) given to outstanding girls who are leaders in dances and other youthful activities. Sometimes the names outlast the youthful period.
bwola	:	the main chiefly royal dance in which the chieftainship drums are used. Each male dancer carries a small drum and drums it to rhythm as the moves dictate.
chamtunu	:	a type of fish found in the Nile and its tributaries.
dakika	:	the minute, from Arabic/Ki-Nubi, (degiga)
Dee-Pee	:	the D.P - Democratic Party.
elektik	:	a villager's way of saying "electric(ity)". In Acholi belief, lightning is a living cock that lives in the sky and is reputed to breed in some chiefs' granaries. It descends to hit targets that have 'problems' reputedly directed to it magically by an evil person.
Evangęli	:	the evangelical books, especially of the Roman Catholic Christian sects.
Gomęs	:	a Goan tailor in Uganda, once created a high-sleeved dress with a massive wraparound for the fattish Baganda matrons. It was the Missionary version of the Victorian ladies' dress. The tailor was called Gomes. The dress has remained bearing his name.
Iboole	:	'Get up and continue'. A cry to hunters and warriors to mark the end of a short rest period. (Iboole may be a Nilo-Hamitic word; it is not a common Acholi word.)

109

Itongo-ten	:	'Stop and rest' - or is it 'cut a rest log'? The cry that permits hunters and warriors to stop for a short rest.
Jok	:	A genetic name for Gods - of the shrine, of the chieftainship shrine, of the hunting ground shrine, or the evil ones are associated with plagues of various kinds.
Kabaka	:	the king of the Baganda.
Kaffir	:	both in Islam and Christianity believers in indigenous religions are referred to derogatively as kaffirs. The Dutch in South Africa extended its meaning to cover all Blacks.
kanju	:	a long robe; Swahili word for Arabic jallabia.
kituba	:	a banyan tree.
Kommunis	:	Communist, Communism. The D.P used to charge the U.P.C of Communism or Communist tendencies.
Kongres	:	Uganda Peoples' Congress.
labikka	:	an annual plant, one metre high (at most) that produces a bunch of black dart-like seeds that stick on people's clothes. (Black-jack) Useable for scouring pus from the eye.
labwori	:	a tree that has bitter bark, but is good fuel when completely dry.
lachoi	:	alcoholic beverage brewed from grains and fermented flour. It is sucked through small pipes with a sieve at the beer-end.

110

lachukuchuku : castanets made from the gourds of fruit trees filled with stones or other musical seeds (pinna-seeds).

lakalachede : extremely small fishes, sometimes one inch long and an eighth of an inch thick. You need a lot to make a dish. But very 'sweet'.

La-loyo (maber) : A new title the Acholi invented for their paramount Chief to counter Baganda 'Kabaka'. It means: 'The good ruler'. A laudable wish expression!

Lamoko-owang : A vigorous youth dance; also known as larakaraka. In the past it was called oling. "The porridge is burnt" - the girl left it on fire to go and have a turn at a dance - but took longer to return: so - "The porridge was burnt":- lamoko-owang.

Larakaraka : onomatopoeic sound of the percussion instruments made from half gourds hit by a bunch of bicycle spokes. (Another name for orak dance.)

lawala : a hoop game; the hoop, a foot in diametre, is hurled through the air, as if it was a bird or animal, and the opposite team had to bring it down by scoring bull.

Lawino : A girl born with natural fold(s) wino on the neck: These are marks of beauty in Acholi culture. But Lawino is also bright, active, lively, intelligent and cultured.

luchoro : a tree with podded red seeds that are used in playing a counting game. It is good for carving and making mortars. But not so good for fuel.

lukut	:	a beverage concocted as treats by grandmothers from the remains of beer, millet or maize meal, and sesame condiment boiled over the fire.
lurono	:	a climbing plant whose root has a flesh the size of a Bic-pen and pith the size of the Bic-ink container. The flesh of the root is sweet-sour. When youth chew a lot of it they forget hunger.
malakwang	:	edible green hibiscus leaves. Unseasoned it tastes revolting and keeps the teeth on. Seasoned with sesame or groundnuts - when its teeth are broken - it is savoury and one of the best greens.
moi	:	moi-names are indicators that their owners have killed a human being. In ages past, among the Nilo-Hamites, one needed such a proof of bravery before one could marry.
mushenji	:	mangy dogs - or half-breed dogs. Derogative term to refer to mixed(human) breeds.
mwaka	:	Swahili word for 'year'. It has been adopted by the Acholi, brought by the educating missionaries from the coast and Buganda.
nanga	:	the lyre whose strings extend over a half-metre long by four inches wide wooden troph. Played by the fingers, sometimes inside a calabash as a loud-speaker.
obuga	:	leaves of a wild herb, bitter to taste.
Ochol	:	name of the antagonist of Lawino. But Ochol also means 'black' so symbolically 'Ochol' represents "the Blacks": Africans, Negroes.

Odude	:	one of the inimical *joks*.
odugu	:	a tree that is hard wood and good for fuel.
Odure	:	a selfishly greedy boy, (or man) who sits by the cooking pot to make sure his wife does not eat some of the meat while cooking.
Odung'e	:	period when grains are ripening.
ogali	:	a hard wood tree, good for firewood, whose soft bark cures wounds, maponya tree.
ogodo	:	a matronly dance for elderly women, rhythmical as if choreographed by a physical training expert. The girl's version is called "*a piti*" i.e "A.P.T"., = A Physical Training Dance. Some policeman or soldier must have invented it for policemen's or army men's wives.
Omara	:	one of the harmful *joks*.
omel	:	the long-whiskered, big-headed, smooth-bodied Nile perch.
omwombye	:	a creeping plant whose bitter roots are chewed or pounded and drunk as cure for many ailments.
opok	:	a hard-wood tree whose bole is used as chief and side pillars, as well as fuel; the bark is used by the Acholi as a hive.
orak	:	a vigorous youth dance, it is for romance in the evening as well as weddings: short form of *larakaraka*.

113

otole	:	a serious mock-war dance the Acholi engage in, taken from their neighbours the Nilo-Hamites to the east. It is the sort of thing one could convert from deadly exercises when one decides to live at peace with into one's past enemies.
Owin	:	(Short for "Lawino") The protagonist of *Wer pa Lawino*. A tall, beautiful girl with a long neck that has natural folds or 'laces' *(wino)* from birth or youth on it. She should be lively, active and all-round useful.
oywelo	:	a tree with black seeds that are eaten when ripe. The pith is spat out. Though it grows tall, its bole is weak and useless for building or cooking.
Pipul Kongres	:	Uganda Peoples' Congress - to the uneducated ear it sounds like that.
poto kot	:	'the falling of rain': the commencement of the rainy season.
Rubang'a	:	the generic word for a Luo God which the Roman Catholics adopted as name for Christian God. (The Anglicans did the same but spelt theirs as *Lubang'a)*. In its native existence *Rubang'a* is a pestilential Jok that breaks people's spinal cords and leaves them humped-backed! (The Hausa call the 'Lord Almighty': Ubangiji. 'Ubangiji' has lately popped up as a personal name in Ruanda!)
seconda	:	second.
Uhuru or uuru	:	the Swahili word for 'freedom'. There is no single and all embrasive word for 'freedom' in Acholi language. For the idea

114

or concept was not familiar or in constant use: the chiefs ruled. You could not be "free" of them! "Loch-ken" is the nearest concept: self-rule.

You-Pee-See   U.P.C - the Uganda Peoples' Congress. I reproduced the sound of the initials in order to illustrate its meaninglessness to Lawino.

Printed in the United States
123792LV00001B/577-612/A